Roy Fisher

Also by Roy Fisher:

The Ship's Orchestra (Fulcrum Press), 1966
Collected Poems 1968 (Fulcrum), 1968
Matrix (Fulcrum), 1971
The Cut Pages (Fulcrum), 1971 (Reissued Oasis / Shearsman, 1986)
The Thing About Joe Sullivan (Carcanet), 1978
Poems 1955 - 1980 (Oxford University Press), 1980
A Furnace (OUP), 1986
Poems 1955 - 1987 (OUP), 1988
Birmingham River (OUP), 1994
The Dow Low Drop — New and Selected Poems (Bloodaxe Books), 1996

Interviews Through Time
& Selected Prose

Roy Fisher

Shearsman Books
2000

First published in Great Britain in 2000 by
Shearsman Books, Lark Rise, Fore Street, Kentisbeare, Devon EX15 2AD.

Distributed in the UK by Oasis Books, 12 Stevenage Road, London SW6
6ES and by Peter Riley (Books), 27 Sturton Street, Cambridge CB1 2QG.
and in the U.S.A. by Small Press Distribution,
1341 Seventh Avenue, Berkeley, CA 94710-1409.
Email: orders@spdbooks.org.   Website: http://www.spdbooks.org.

ISBN 0 907562 26 4

Printed and bound in the U.K. by
The Book Factory, 35-37 Queensland Rd., London N7 7AN.

Acknowledgements and Publishing History:
The *Talks for Words* were first broadcast on the BBC Radio 3 series *Words* in 1977-
1978. All six (including the fourth talk which is not reprinted here) were later collected
as a chapbook by Blackweir Press, Cardiff. The interview with Jed Rasula and the late
Mike Erwin first appeared in *Nineteen Poems and an Interview* (Grosseteste, Pensnett,
Staffs., 1975). The interview with John Tranter originally appeared in the web magazine
jacket (www.jacket.zip.com.au) in 1996. Peter Robinson's 1977 interview first appeared
in *Granta*. His 1998 interview is presented here for the first time, with the permission
of the participants. The interview with Eric Mottram first appeared in *Saturday Morning*
1 (ed. Simon Pettet, London, 1976) and is reprinted here by permission of the estate of
Eric Mottram, which is managed by King's College, London University. The interview
with Robert Sheppard first appeared in *Gargoyle* 24 (Washington, D.C.) and was later
republished as a chapbook by Toads Damp Press, London, 1986. *Roy Fisher on Roy
Fisher* originally appeared in *The Rialto*. The list of interviews is reprinted here from
Derek Slade's comprehensive bibliography with permission of the compiler. The editor
is grateful to Roy Fisher, Jed Rasula, John Tranter, Robert Sheppard, Peter Robinson,
Derek Slade and the administrators of Eric Mottram's estate at King's College London
for their kind permission to reprint previously published material. The *Antebiography*
was first published in the *Contemporary Authors Autobiography Series* by Gale Research
Inc., Detroit. The cover, reproduced by permission of Roy Fisher, shows a street party
in Kentish Road, in 1938. Roy Fisher is the eighth child from the front on the right side
of the table. Inside the front cover: the author playing the piano in 1979, © Roy Fisher.

Contents

Introduction

The origin of this book lies in my conviction that Roy Fisher's interviews, all of which are now very difficult to find, contained a great deal of information that would be of use to readers and students of his work and should therefore once again be made available. The interviews that had hitherto been published—the majority of them between 1970 and 1985—tended to concentrate on the his earlier work, and thus arose the idea of commissioning a new interview which would concentrate on the period starting with the publication of *A Furnace*. This was long overdue, given that *A Furnace* is by common consent Roy Fisher's *magnum opus*, at least so far.

Our concern throughout was to focus on poetics, with a little biographical leavening, and the interviews that have been plundered to make up this narrative were chosen with that in view. This is no reflection on the other interviews, which often covered the same themes or were, for various reasons, more ephemeral in nature. Each of them in fact has something to offer, but those selected here offered more and enabled us to avoid too much elision from one interview to another. Simply republishing the originals as they had appeared would of course have led to innumerable overlaps and anachronisms. In view of this we decided that a cut-and-paste approach would be the better option and would serve to lend an air of narrative logic to the whole proceedings, especially when combined with the *Antebiography* which opens this volume. The new interview with Peter Robinson, which was commissioned especially for this book, appears here in its entirety, however. Having reached this stage, it was clear too that the review of his own book *The Dow Low Drop* that Roy had written for the magazine *The Rialto* also fitted well into the overall scheme of things, and made an amusing conclusion to the narrative that had been constructed.

Five of the BBC *Talks for Words* are also included—the original fourth *Talk* was left out as the author was dissatisfied with it—because these represent more of Roy Fisher talking, albeit more formally, and at the same time form one of the very few prose pieces that he has allowed to see the light of day. They were worth rescuing from oblivion.

Tony Frazer
January 2000.

Antebiography

I must have been conceived during those days in late 1929 when Wall Street was falling in ruins; I was a latecomer in a poor but prudent family which thought itself complete, and although nobody ever hinted as much to me, I can see now that my birth, in June 1930, will have been accompanied by a revival of economic fear and some privation. These were to last until the arrival of the prosperity which the war of 1939 brought to working people. My father was a craftsman, working for the same small, paternalist jewellery firm ("Walter, you're a good workman, and if you ever leave here I'll see to it that you never get another job anywhere in this trade") to which he'd been apprenticed at fourteen, in 1903. It was a luxury trade which withered with the Depression and took a long while to recover; my father was to earn far better wages when the war came, but for assembling aircraft, not setting diamonds. The fact that he then felt it demeaning to become for a while just another factory worker, even for three times the pay, tells something about the family ethos.

Not that he actually enjoyed making jewellery, even though he did take a certain pride in his minute skill: he was in it only because he had been put to it as a boy. Jewellery of some sort had been the family trade for at least three generations; they'd lived in a succession of homes never more than walking distance from the same nest of small workshops just outside the city centre. This was the Jewellery Quarter, a congested patch maybe three quarters of a mile square on the crest of Hockley Hill. It was the archetype, almost a concentrate, of the Birmingham system of proliferating small manufactures which developed through the eighteenth and nineteenth centuries. The "masters" would start by having their workshops attached to their houses, all over the district; the workshops would extend piecemeal to cram the backyards, then the gardens. At that stage the master would move his family a mile or two out to a new suburb, and every room of the original house would be filled with workbenches or clerks' desks. There were hundreds of these establishments in Hockley, dark and chaotic, their work spaces linked by rickety stairways and catwalks. It was an area I saw for the first time only in my teens, working as a telegram delivery boy one school holiday; certainly my father never saw any reason to take me there, and although I once called at W.H. Small's front office with a message when he was in hospital, I never set eyes on the room where, apart from the two wars, he spent every working day for over fifty years. It's quite likely that my mother never learned exactly where the place was.

I think my father would probably have been better suited by temperament to some sort of clerical, white-collar job; he was certainly literate enough. But that would have meant, under the crazy but insidiously effective English system, changing social classes; and for the large family of my grandfather (also Walter Fisher) the game was one of consolidation rather than movement upward. Nobody was put to an education involving expense which future fortune might or might not repay; that would be the plan for my own generation, once the consolidation had taken effect. That family—Lizzie, Ern,

Wal, Doris, Jessie, Rose, Albert, Florrie—earned their livings early. My uncle Ern was the only one ever to become his own boss, and that was in a very small way, as half of a two-man japanning business he ran in partnership with his sister Florrie's husband, Will, but which neither of them owned.

I write of that household as being my grandfather's partly as a fact of memory, for my grandmother was dead three years before before I was born; but by every account, the setup had always been patriarchal, right from the elder Walter's marriage in 1885, at nineteen (twenty-one on the marriage lines), to Mary Jane Kite. She was two years older, living a few doors away in James Street, Lozells, and on the point of giving birth to my Aunt Lizzie. When I came to know him—or rather to witness him, for he didn't have much interest in children—he was an impressive old man, bald, lean, and hard, with a down-turned moustache and an outfit that included polished leather leggings and made him look more like a shepherd or a stockman dressed up for market day than a man who had spent all his life within a couple of miles of the centre of Birmingham. He was a little bowed, but loping and agile. He stank of tobacco smoke, and his speech was a direct, articulate Old Brummagem, a strong, railing accent, very different from the sodden and nondescript English usually thought of nowadays as the local language. Just by his presence he dominated any room he was in, though I don't remember him as interacting with other people much; for his last ten years or so he was accompanied everywhere by his retriever, which both served as an intimate and did all his socialising for him. You could make contact with him via the dog; and he'd usually give the children a few of the dog's chocolate drops, when the dog had had enough. I was brought up to think of him as something of a household tyrant and a miser, and there was probably some truth in both. He certainly had an unusually large amount of savings for a retired working man who had raised a big family: when he died in 1945 he left over a thousand pounds, enough to buy outright a couple of houses of the sort we were then living in for a rent of ten shillings a week.

He never moved from the house, 77 Anglesey Street, Lozells, in which he'd spent most of his adult life. It was a plain brick street of terrace houses, without bay windows or front gardens, and it ran down from the Lozells Road, which was something of a shopping street, into the factory-filled valley east of Hockley; beyond that, the hill rose by way of Great King Street, where he'd been born, to the Jewellery Quarter, where he worked. In the other direction, away from the city centre, he would in his earlier years have come quickly into open country; and that was the clue to the other side of his life. At the time of his birth, Great King Street will have been almost at the edge of the built-up area, and the other places he lived in—all within a square half-mile or so of one another—were in the zone to which the edge of town had pushed itself by the time he married; James Street looked out into farmland. Once he was settled in Anglesey Street, the suburbs went on spreading beyond him, a good ten miles more, till they almost met, as they now do meet, Walsall, the next town. He didn't, however, do what many small householders did, his own father among them: cultivate his backyard and an allotment garden as well. Although a complete product of the city and its economy, he didn't at all, as far as I know, *use* the city, and feed off its atmospheres and opportunities in the way really urbanised people do. Whenever he could, he got out.

He was exactly of the generation of working men who were liberated by the safety bicycle back into the countryside from which their parents or grandparents had probably come. He took his holidays and weekend excursions in male company or alone, by bicycle, covering considerable distances. And the machines he rode were the only extravagance he had. He would have them built to his specifications: not racers, but well-engineered, rugged road cycles. The last of them came to my father as a premature legacy, and quickly to me; it was so heavily constructed that the old man could hardly move it. I found it hard work, too: a smooth, black brute with a broad, sprung saddle, oil-bath chain guard and so much equipment of one sort and another slung low on its bodywork that it would almost stand up by itself.

As he grew older he restricted himself more and more to an old haunt nearer town, the wide stretch of protected wild heath and woodland called Sutton Park, in Sutton Coldfield. He would get away through the suburbs into that. He had been a noted swimmer in the pools there, particularly in the depths of winter, belonging to a group of ice-breaking swimmers; their successors probably still swim for the Walter Fisher Cup, a winter trophy. And it was in that park that he met his death, early in 1945. Since the deaths of my aunt Lizzie and her family in an air raid (this was the incident described in my poem 'The Entertainment of War') he'd become more and more remote and confused; there were perpetual ringing noises in his head. His trouble was probably tinnitus, but the general opinion—which he may have shared—was that he was losing his wits as he approached eighty. He didn't come visiting any more, communicated with people very little, and finally didn't stir from the house, as if in a terminal feebleness. One January day, he disappeared, and the dog with him. Late the next day, and a dozen miles away in Sutton Park, the dog led a passerby to where he lay dying of exposure after a freezing night. I think everybody considered it a good death for him. Uncle Ern and my father cycled out to the park with his ashes, no doubt strapped to the carrier of his own massive bicycle, and scattered them near Blackroot Pool.

The style of all the Fishers was one of alert, short-range attention; humour was brisk and dismissive, even abrupt. Their voices could be sharp or declamatory, and their movements and facial expressions tended to the vigorous and, on occasion, manic. They coped with life as they went along, and on the level they found themselves on. Constitutionally, they kept their noses clean and a little money in the bank. Of my grandfather's children, none, so far as I know, ever faced insolvency, traumatic unemployment, or breakdown; none engaged in crime; none met with a great increase in fortune, or went looking for such a thing. When they came to have taller, better-educated children, electric light, and indoor lavatories, it was only at the pace at which those things came to many other people. They didn't direct themselves much to the future, and spent little time reminiscing—mostly, I think, because the past had been so harsh they didn't enjoy thinking about it. Of my grandfather's numerous brothers and sisters, for instance, I only ever heard one talked about, and that in long retrospect. This was Great-Uncle John, who was uncharacteristic. Born in 1859, he made the move away from manual work two generations early, becoming the first qualified "high-speed typewriter" in Birmingham. He then married into a Catholic family; his wife was judged to have been a woman of some pretensions; and on her he begot, it was said, three headmistresses. Dominated by his womenfolk, he became eccentrically speculative, and would happily give his money away; I suppose he was a steady hypomanic. At any rate, his family consigned him to institutions from time to time. But for the rest, virtually everything I know about them from the time before I was born comes not from anecdote but from searching the public records. In 1861, my great grandfather William Fisher, an electroplater (probably working in the bulkier end of the jewellery trade) was recorded as living in Great King Street with his wife, Georgina Mason, and their six children (and there were more to come, including my grandfather) in a household headed by her mother, a widow born in Hornton in Oxfordshire and working as a mangler. The Kites and the other tributary family, the Mousleys, were almost certainly already in the same parish somewhere. Ann Mason and her husband had arrived in the city around 1825, to work as button-makers. Both came from families settled as far back as records go—to around 1600—in a tight clutch of villages in the rolling country around Edge Hill: Avon Dassett, Burton Dassett, Hornton, Fenny Compton. Unvaryingly, the occupations had been in or close to farming, with a slow decline in status and possessions.

I never heard of any of the Fishers having any political allegiance, nor any trace of felt religion. My father would describe his father as having been a Freethinker, but I think that just meant he was a sceptic. There exist photographs of my father and his brother Ern as young men, in a Methodist cricket team; there are also photographs of them, from the same period, in a Church of England football eleven. My father also passed the most exalted period of his life as a boy chorister at that same church. The religion seemed to have no effect on him, but socially the church choir affected him a good deal. For one thing, it came close to removing him from his family, from his class, and from Birmingham. That was when, as head chorister and principal soloist, he was talent-spotted for the choir of Canterbury Cathedral with, I suppose, the offer of a free scholarship to the Cathedral Choir School and all the opportunities for social mobility that would carry with it. For some reason, my grandfather didn't give his consent; the refusal wasn't thought to be out of character. At any rate, my father stayed on at Saint Mary's, Handsworth, for as long as his voice lasted, and beyond: far from being eager to drop his register and come out as a man, he wanted to preserve his position, and the excitement of singing the high line, long past the natural time. He forced his voice to stay up till it was a falsetto, probably ruining any prospect of having a reasonable adult singing voice. He certainly never acquired anything more than a rather strained tenor, and as a man didn't sing much. In a rare moment of reminiscence he once gave me the best possible summary of his relationship with my grandfather. "I only ever heard my father sing once," he said; "I came home early, and as I came up the entry I heard a man singing in a most beautiful tenor voice. And that was my dad. And when he heard me he stopped, and then pretended he hadn't been doing it. I never heard him do it again."

Saint Mary's choir was an interesting choice. Handsworth was then an altogether leafier and more affluent place than Lozells, and Saint Mary's was several churches away from my father's home territory. He must have been drawn there by an ambition to sing in the strongest team. The church was the handsome medieval parish church of an independent Staffordshire borough, not annexed by Birmingham till 1911, and at that time one of the districts where the manufacturers had their mansions and the clerical and business classes their villas. It was a place of parlour maids and tennis courts, and the quality came to church in carriages. The church itself had numerous clergy, a huge choir, and was a centre of social power; at the same time it had—as it still has—something of the atmosphere of a village church, sandstone-built and set in a spacious graveyard under a canopy of tall trees. It embodied the English tradition which the industrial nineteenth century was reaching for, inventing where necessary and taking to itself as a talisman; and I'm sure its sub-Gothic dignities had a strong and romantic effect on my father's imagination. It didn't prompt him to social climbing, but was more of an escapism, allied to the old man's cycle rides, which he often shared.

One of the local girls who sat in the front pew and made eyes at the choirboys was a jobbing gardener's daughter called Emma—or Pem, the only person I've ever heard of with that name—Jones. Their courtship turned out to be long: they were married in Saint Mary's in the autumn of 1918, by which time she was twenty-seven and my father twenty-nine, a signals lance-corporal in the London Fusiliers on leave from France. But my father's careful pencil drawing of the church was already in her autograph album by the time he was a sixteen-year-old jeweller's apprentice and boy soprano and she was just starting work in a small sweetshop in the area everybody called "the village," the group of shops round the old toll bar in Villa Road, about midway between her family territory and his.

Whereas the Fishers seem to have been established on their small patch for generations, the Joneses were new arrivals in Handsworth. They'd lived for a time near Harborne, further round the semirural western edge of the city, and my grandfather Edward Jones had at some time worked for the Chamberlain family: possibly Joseph, the creator of the modern Birmingham; certainly Austen, who became Foreign Secretary. My grandmother Emma Westwood had had some family connection with a laundry business and had done housekeeping work in one of the smaller outlying hospitals; I have the impression that she'd also been in domestic service. Something of that sort was certainly the family style, which was in marked contrast to that of the Fishers; the contrast was worked out year after year in the household I grew up in, and it made an uncomfortable inheritance. The Joneses had the air of servants who'd been paid off, given their freedom, and who weren't too happy with the bargain; life was an ache, a trial to be faced with cheerfulness and charm amid slowly declining fortunes. I don't know whether this air of decline was based in anything substantial. The Joneses didn't reminisce any more than did the Fishers; and although their thoughts seemed to be turned towards the past, they were thoughts that lay too deep for tears, or words. Usually, at any rate; I can remember seeing my mother and my aunts weeping for times gone by. And there was always something wistful about the charm and the cheerfulness. There was certainly nothing of the bluff pugnacity of the Fishers.

This was, of course, the mood I learned to know in the thirties, and it may be that the one focus of reminiscence and overt regret which they had was the real cause of the pervading wistfulness. This was the loss of Ivy Cottage, something which happened quite a few years before I was born. Somehow, on arriving in Handsworth around the turn of the century, the family had gained the tenancy of an idyllic old yeoman cottage, left marooned in woodland and among fields as the prosperous suburb developed all round it; and there they seem to have lived an almost rural life for a quarter of a century. In speech and manner they gave the impression of being country people, and by preserving that style for so long within a couple of miles of the city centre, they seemed also to be preserving a pre-industrial past. It was only when they lost Ivy Cottage—the story went that they were in some way tricked out of the lease— that they had to become urbanised. Even so, Howard Road, to which they had moved by the time I was born, was far from being a harsh city street. It was a quiet little cut-through, with varied housing, mostly quite old, and a small farmhouse and yard still tucked away behind the houses. But Ivy Cottage had been a complete survival, with climbing roses, old brickwork, and a pump in the yard. It sat among its birch trees half a mile or so up beyond Saint Mary's, and I suppose that for my father it was a powerful additional magic to be added to whatever the church gave him.

The other contrast to the life he was used to lay in the fact that the Jones family was emphatically matriarchal. My soulful-eyed grandmother ran things, persuasively and without resistance. She did it mostly from her bed in later years. My grandfather Edward Jones I knew as a slow, sweet-natured old man, white-bearded, straw-hatted, and with distant blue eyes: the type-figure of a retired gardener. I was told he'd been perhaps a little less uncomplicated in earlier years, before a fall through a hothouse roof and a crack on the head; there was no knowing. He outlived my grandmother by ten years, but didn't liberate himself from his chimney-corner existence.

The family wasn't a matriarchy of the strong sort where daughters breed daughters and men are peripheral; it was a home base near the end of a line, and it exerted a steady, soft, sweet magnetism. When my mother used the word "home" we knew that she meant—although she'd never lived in it—her parents' house in Howard Road. My grandparents had five children, four of whom lived to adulthood, and of those four only my mother married and had children. Her elder sister Elsie worked from home as a dressmaker to the local well-to-do, and became, when past child-bearing, the third wife of an elderly *rentier* who lived opposite, enjoying, while she lasted, the slight elevation of position which had come to her by way of a little patience. My mother herself was to marry quite late. Uncle Ted, a bighearted, affectionate bachelor, who worked as a builder's labourer, died in his middle forties, a few months after his mother. The youngest, Ethel, born in 1900, was by general agreement pampered and brought up to idleness, after which she spent thirty years or so keeping house for her parents till they died. She went out to work, cleaning and then doing light factory work, only when she was near retiring age; she never married.

I've said that the contrast between the styles of the Fishers and the Joneses made for an uncomfortable inheritance. On the credit side, the Joneses' quasi-rural nostalgia combined with my father's inherited commitment to country excursions to provide, through my childhood, blissful, almost visionary experiences on outings and walks, supported by an unshakable moral faith in something called Nature. That basic guidance, and many of those experiences have stayed with me all my life. There are people who know me for my writings about urban landscapes and city life and who find it impossible to square that knowledge with the fact that I now live, not as a lifelong denizen of those streets, but in a quite remote and wild place in the Derbyshire hills. But it's the paradox I was given as a child—the sensation of having been born in a state of exile from some unknown countryside—which forced me to stare so hard at all the particulars of my city surroundings.

The real discomfort was social, a matter of loyalties and emotional allegiances. My father was probably the least matter-of-fact, the most reflective of the Fishers; he would need to be, to marry into the Jones family, into which he fitted quite well, though as the years went by, he grew impatient and dismissive about what he considered their passivity, and the uselessness of their little bits of gentility. By the time I was born he probably saw much more of my mother's family than he did of his own. We children certainly did. Visits to Grandpa Fisher's house in Anglesey Street came once or twice a year, so that it felt physically like a foreign territory, whereas the Jones house in Howard Road was a home from home, visited on many weekends and filled with familiar objects and sensations. Being brought up close to my mother—and she was by nature possessive of her two sons—I absorbed, without explicit teaching, the very strong sense that the Jones way was the true way, and that the Fisher way was the way of a heartless world with no leaves on the trees, no flowers in the vases, and sharp edges everywhere. There was no enmity between the families—simply the assumption, from my mother's side, of an inherent incompatibility. And when my parents were at odds, usually about money, the incompatibility of the clans became personal: my father was characterised as a hot-tempered miser, my mother as a devious and indulgent spendthrift. These were just the positions they repeatedly took up; the money there was to argue over was pathetically little. But the slogans of those occasional wars made their impression on me.

My mother was thirty-nine and my father forty-one when I was born. And for our sort of people those were advanced ages for childbearing. My sister was ten years, and my brother eight years my senior; and my parents seemed much older in relation to me than did those of other children. My mother, for instance, was prematurely grey: I never knew her with dark hair. And my father was bald, with nothing boyish about his demeanour. And I came to realise—though not really until I reached that time of life myself—that they were both by then in quite poor shape and had their troubles. They did well to be as animated as they were. I don't think for instance, that giving me birth had done my mother any good at all. She didn't always walk well, couldn't go up or down stairs except one step at a time, and already had the beginnings of a tremor which plagued her later years.

As for my father, I think now that he was an uncompensated war casualty. After volunteering, being rejected as unfit because of a cartilage injury, and undergoing surgery to make himself eligible for service, he spent three years in the trenches, an experience about which he had little to say. He didn't set any value on it, or on his campaign medals or on the results of the Allies' victory. Physically, he was a fairly small man, and I imagine he must always have been nervous, tensed like a spring; on the football field he'd been a fast wing forward, and at cricket a ferociously fast bowler. The stress of his war service, and the problems and frustrations which followed it, will have damaged him. By the time I knew him, there was not an atom of relaxation in him, most of the time. He'd continued with his sports past the age when it would have been sensible to stop, and had pushed himself too far. He was in frequent pain from rheumatism and stomach ulcers, and he slept badly. His thyroid had become seriously overactive and he repeatedly refused the surgery which was the only available treatment. He was hard for a child to get to know; much of what I thought of as his personality, the signs I read him by, must have been the phenomenology of his illness: the losses of temper, the over-loud laughter, the friendliness that seemed far more forced and uneasy than it was. It alarmed me, I suppose, and distanced me from him, and it never occurred to me to model my behaviour on his in any way. When I took to doing things I'd learned from him, like roaming the countryside, on foot or bicycle, I arrogantly assumed I was doing it my way; and it was with real astonishment that I discovered, in adulthood, that it was his face I'd inherited more than my mother's. I'd ruled out any such possibility.

It's easy for me to see my whole character, and the course of my life, as determined by an early disposition to be, quietly and without fuss, as unlike him as possible in the way I did things. Where he was keen, quick and hyperactive, I grew up to be laid back, noncommittal, sceptical about the value of any action at all. This scepticism was strengthened by the spectacle of the fascinating but turbulent adolescent years of my sister and brother.

And I grew secretive. This wasn't purely temperamental. Either parent would sound me out about what the other might be thinking or doing. I didn't like that; but it taught me that the discovery of others' plans, motives, and feelings was a powerful currency. In consequence, I became disinclined fully to confide anything in anybody, a habit which was to stay with me long after it was of any possible tactical use. A few years ago I made a note: "My life is the history of my secrets." Which meant, not that my secrets ever amounted to anything, but that my whole sense of myself was as a carrier of secrets. Early on, I'd decided that if secrets spelled safety, the best course for me was to *be* a secret incarnate. Good for the contemplative life, if in a warped way; bad for the active.

And when the active life hit me, when I went at five to Wattville Road School, I was unprepared for it. I'd had the upbringing many youngest children receive, being capably but unconcernedly looked after by an experienced mother who was busy with the still-unfamiliar challenges generated by the older children. I was just kept close to my mother; the other people I met for five years were mostly relatives, and mostly adults. I had very little contact with other children. So my first day at school, when I suddenly encountered what felt like the whole of the rest of the human race, was a shock. I still haven't got over it. Something had got at all those children and brutalised them. They were loud and aggressive—even their friendliness was intrusive—and they were even more taboo-ridden than I was. Even when they didn't seem intelligent, they behaved as if far more worldly-wise than me. Since I was never worldly-wise, and not rebellious in an active way, I was always to be puzzled by the way the world seemed to run on taboos and bans, a life defined by its negatives. My parents, without any theology beyond a sentimental attachment to the church where they'd met, often seemed to have devised a secular Calvinism, overhung with calamity to come, a calamity in and of the world.

I hated school, apart from one or two encouraging relationships with teachers when I was ten or eleven, and I learned to survive in a paradoxical way—I soon found out that I was better than most, if not all, of the others at the lessons; and I could sing and draw, though I'm lefthanded and writing was an agony, particularly with steel pens and filthy ink. I had no talent for naughtiness, and so had all the qualifications of a teacher's pet. Insofar as I wanted to, I could always have a secure place close to the seat of authority, crazy as that authority might seem. At the same time, I had no standing in the playground, a place which always seemed to me a chaos of violence and spite. Out there, I was for years "the Daft Kid," the slow-on-the-uptake, the dim-witted. And since that was my name, that was who I believed I was. The knowledge that I always beat them all at schoolwork was a palliative, but no more. They were reality, after all. I was never without friends, but they were drawn from the quieter end of the mob. The rougher end was something to worry about: it had some wild and violent characters from down beyond the railway tracks, and I came to rely on my acquired persona as a talisman for physical safety—"Let him alone, he's only the Daft Kid."

The railway line was a real, as well as a notional, boundary in the patch of ground where I grew up—a landmark which was in fact made by its shape and the uses it had in those days, into a moralized landscape. That edge of Handsworth is an easy slope running down from the ridge carrying the Birmingham-Holyhead road and into Winson Green and Smethwick, at whose conjunction Matthew Boulton's Soho Foundry stood. Wattville Road (there never was a place called Wattville, though it may once have been projected) is a straight track from top to bottom of that slope, with the main railway line which leads northwest out of the city centre three miles away crossing it halfway down; the school is the last thing before the railway bridge as you go down. The zone above the railway was mainly given over to streets of fairly tidy terraced houses; these included Kentish Road, where I was born and lived until I was twenty-three. And up beyond those streets were newer houses, a park, sports grounds, a huge semirural municipal cemetery, and a patch of farmland. But below the railway, the hill seemed to steepen, dropping among slum houses to a valley bottom filled with all the gigantic signs of heavy industry: chimney stacks, black and rusting factory buildings, huge gasholders, a pandemonium of metallic noise, a network of oily, green canals. The whole place was threatening, harsh, and mysterious. Also it was a zone to which we had no entrée, since my father worked a good way nearer town, in the Jewellery Quarter.

We were out there on the western edge of Handsworth by way of a temporary expedient which turned permanent. When my father came out of the army in 1919, he and my mother, then pregnant, lodged in the house, 74 Kentish Road, rented by his sister Lizzie and her husband. It was well away from either Jones or Fisher territory. Before long, Lizzie's family moved, first to a house in the same street, then eventually to the house down on the edge of Smethwick, where they were all to be killed twenty years later. My parents took on the tenancy of 74; their three children were born there and they themselves stayed there till they died, my father in 1959 and my mother in 1965.

Kentish Road was in a small edge-of-town development of four uniform terraced streets, built some time between 1900 and 1910. Originally they had backed onto pastureland, but that had been taken over by the sports field and timber yard of the Birmingham Carriage and Wagon Company, whose main gate was at the bottom of our street and whose territory occupied the whole of the southern outlook from our backyard. It made a decent, docile, politically conservative working-class district which at that time showed hardly anything of the raw impulse towards affluence which was to drive almost all the inhabitants to flee from it in the fifties. When I was a child, many of the adults around me had been born in vile slums; it was as if they were resting for a generation before moving on. It was a quiet, tired, fatalistic place, where the people made great efforts to establish and guard their privacy. There was very little of the proverbial working-class habit of being always in and out of one another's houses.

Our house was small, though I've lived in bigger ones that felt smaller. It had a tiny garden at the front, with a domed bush of yellow privet and a border of bluebells. There was a narrow hall, and a front parlour with a piano and an archaic three-piece suite. The living room had a deal table with a green chenille cloth, a blackleaded range, again with a chenille valance round its high mantelpiece, on which stood a polished brass shellcase and other ornaments. There was an old blue basket chair, and the remains of a suite upholstered in green and red. Down one step was the narrow little kitchen containing a stone sink with the house's one tap, a built-in copper boiler, a small range fireplace, a black gas cooker, a mangle that folded to make a table, and, in wet weather, my father's and my brother's bicycles. There was a canary in a cage, my father's pet; and outside in the blue-brick-paved yard he had others – fish in an aquarium on a stand, and a large wall-mounted cage for a song thrush. Along the yard were a coal house and a toilet with a scrubbed plank seat.The house was a set of closed compartments, in which it was possible for the five of us to have some seclusion from one another when we wanted it, if not from the neighbours, whose noise came through the walls on either side regardless. The staircase was hidden behind a door opening off the living room and led to three bedrooms, one very small. The house was lit, rather dimly, by gas, except for the bedrooms, where, since the gas was unreliable, we burned oil. I had a home-made lamp made from a coffee bottle filled with paraffin, with a bootlace for a wick. The whole place was floored with cold linoleum, and there were a couple of home-made rag hearth rugs. There were few books, and we took a newspaper and comics; there were some intensely memorable monochrome framed prints, and four gilt-framed original oil paintings by a local artist; I still have three of them. Nothing much changed in the house till the end of the thirties, when an upturn in the jewellery trade and, probably more significantly, the fact that my sister and brother had left school and were earning, brought electric light and some more modern furniture.

The gardens were the width of the houses, ten or twelve feet, and no more than thirty feet long: they were strips for hanging out washing. My father took ours over and populated it densely with plants and animals. Against the solid sports-field fence he improvised a shed for hens and rabbits; the other fences he raised to head-height with scrap wood from fruit crates and covered them with rambler roses; all the rest of the space was crammed with cottage garden flowers and whatever vegetables there was room for. Beyond the garden, the chief amenity was open sky. The sports field, much of it rough grass, stretched away for half a mile, with the next factory buildings miniaturised beyond it; and to the left, the works timber yard was spacious and remote, with a small locomotive and a couple of steam cranes puffing about in it. I always had one of the bedrooms facing out westwards over this area; there was nothing claustrophobic about being there.

That open view was important. Even more so was the access to the area of countryside which opened up ten minutes' walk away, across the Holyhead road. Although it lay at the city boundary it wasn't open country; that was a couple of hours' bus ride away. The few square miles of land we had, a single shallow valley under a crest of upland, was just a patch that hadn't yet been turned to city uses, lying across the widening stretch between that Holyhead road and the next one to the east, that went on to Stafford and Manchester. The Birmingham suburbs petered out just about where we lived, and gave way to this rather run-down bit of country, which, strangely, didn't go on reaching to the northwest as the roads diverged, but was hemmed in after a few miles by a string of industrial townships which gradually joined up to isolate it. But it was an enclosure whose edges you didn't have to think about, unless you wanted to react to the mysterious sight of sunlit cooling towers rising above a misty horizon ten miles away. It was a vista of fields and copses and rags of hedgerow, stands of tall trees, and the long sandstone wall of what had been the Earl of Dartmouth's estate. Its heart was made up of five or six farms, dominated by a pair of collieries; a railway branch line ran through the fields, and pushing quietly in from the edges were the spacious, landgrabbing outreaches of city life; two lonely golf courses with birch woods and scrub; a public park; the vast cemetery, still mostly unused, and, wherever the houses stopped, allotment gardens packed with weird shanties with their flue-pipes, rain-barrels, and bits of pub window.

So there was no clear distinction between the town and the country. The cemetery and the golf course had wild edges to them, and the desolate reed-bordered pool that was the destination for special excursions lay, with a complete scenic rightness, under the arid, black and red-brown spoil heap of Jubilee Colliery, with its baleful flat top and the deep scars of rain channels running down to the thickets of alder and willow around its base. Nobody ever suggested in my hearing that the collieries or the cemetery or the allotments were "spoiling" the landscape. They were part of it; it was a particular type of countryside that had those things in it.

When I was old enough I would spend, with friends or alone, walking or cycling, a great deal of time there. When I was younger it was a regular Sunday-morning excursion with my father, part of a routine set of activities. We'd walk the lanes while my mother cooked. In the afternoon she'd join us for a strange family party on one of the upper slopes of the cemetery, with sweeping views. A selection of my father's brothers and sisters, their spouses and children—up to a dozen people—would gather at the grave of my grandmother and my Uncle Albert, who'd died young. My grandfather never came. They'd change the flowers in the marble urn, talk for an hour, and disperse. I grew to be quite at home there. When my mother's mother and uncle Ted were buried a couple of hundred yards down the slope, some of us would tend that too. It had a patch of turf, which my father would clip with a pair of kitchen scissors he carried in his pocket.

Sometimes we'd take our walks in the other direction, down into Hell, quiet and sunlit on a Sunday morning. Whereas I took the countryside to be righteous, there was a whiff of addiction about my appetite for the beauty of the great rusting sheds, the tarry stinks, and the slimy canals of Smethwick. It was a lonely and gigantic landscape, with hardly anybody in it.

Until I was in my teens we travelled very little indeed. Each year there'd be a trip or two to the city centre, little more than three miles away, and a day's outing by bus or tram to one of the traditional spots just outside the city—the Lickey Hills, or Kinver Edge. Before I was born, there had been family holidays by the sea, but I was never to go on holiday with my parents. I was thirteen before I slept a night outside Birmingham; and there had probably been only two or three nights away from home in all that time. There were a few day trips to more distant places, so rare and so unreal that they had for me the impact of transcendental spiritual visitations. At six I was taken to the Malverns, and in a neighbour's car to the Vale of Llangollen and the mountains and seacoast of North Wales. The same neighbours later took us to the Vale of Evesham and Dovedale. These places—I didn't know where they were, or why they were as they were—excited me enormously.

I was already reading obsessively, the books coming not from school, where the provision was thin, but from the public library, which I joined shortly after starting school. And I was drawing. I started with a blackboard and coloured chalks, then went on to cover every paper surface that could be provided for me, usually with pencil and crayon drawings, sometimes with watercolour. I was fairly slapdash, but I don't think I conformed for long to what is expected of child artists. I was inspired by the illustrators of adventure stories, historical romances, and by the appearances of things as I saw them at the cinema. All these I set myself to copy, repeating and developing favourite scenes over and over again. The siege of Omdurman in *The Four Feathers*, and episodes from the Errol Flynn *Robin Hood*, Trafalgar, from *Lady Hamilton*. I drew in a sort of panoramic realism, with scores of characters accurately costumed and equipped, and mostly stuck full of spears or arrows.

For years this activity was the most positive thing in my life. It led to the only real lift I got from my school days, something which should, I suppose, have set me on a career as a painter had I been able to seize the advantage. In September 1939, the school had been closed down and most of the children evacuated to the country. My parents elected not to send me, reasoning on my behalf that, were they to be killed, the double bereavement would be more than I could bear, and that hence I would no doubt prefer to be blown to bits along with them. I was told all this at the time, and was persuaded. Early in

1940, the school reopened for the few who remained, and I quickly passed the examination qualifying me to go on to the grammar school when I was old enough, in a year and a half's time. In doing so, I'd virtually exhausted the Wattville Road curriculum and had time to spare. Pop Lewis, my teacher, a shrewd and spirited Welshman, played a hunch and set me up in a corner with a full-sized blackboard and easel, a set of powder colours and brushes, the biggest sheet of paper I'd ever seen, and a commission to paint *The Knights of the Round Table Asleep under the Hill until Britain's Hour of Need*. It took days, and people came to watch. I rose to the challenge. When the picture was hung high on the classroom wall I had a little fame, and the status of court painter. I was excused lessons for long periods to paint subjects of my choice. My range was wide: *The Last Fight of the "Revenge," Marco Polo Setting Out from Venice to Asia, Everyday Life in Ancient Rome, Abraham Leading Isaac Away from the Family Tent to Be Sacrificed, Marco Polo Returning to Venice from Asia*. There was even a street scene, painted from the life. These all hung above the desks, a deep, lengthening frieze. I suppose I had talent. I certainly enjoyed my role, and took it seriously.

Outside the painting, however, there were things starting to go wrong for me. At seven I'd become myopic and had to wear glasses. I took this blow very badly, for it removed me overnight from any hope of normality. We were a family accustomed to dark good looks in youth, and I was now not going to make it. As well as being the Daft Kid I had to join the very small number of children who were patronised, or worse, for having some physical disability. Adults were kind; children, boys and girls alike, were merciless, until the novelty wore off. My outer and inner lives started to drift away from each other. Anxiously overfed by my mother, I grew fat, and stayed so. My life started to move in a series of lurches, between mild hope and mild despair. The war itself had a mixed effect. The air raids of 1940, when I spent many of my nights in the Anderson shelter in the garden, with bombs and equally lethal British shrapnel whistling down, were exciting but appalling, not so much from the fear of a notional death as from the actual presence afterwards of acres of destruction and disorder, the still, featureless mountains of bricks which had been neighbouring streets. After that, my brother and my brother-in-law spent years in danger. I would engage in elaborate daily, muttered rituals, which grew longer and longer, in order to ensure their safety, which I believed depended only on me. At the same time, there was, with the prolongation of stoicism, a deadening of areas of feeling.

Moving to Handsworth Grammar School cheered me up at first. Life was socially more comfortable, and the air of tradition—most of it fairly new in fact—was supportive and seductive for a while. But merely being selected to go there, a mile away from home, isolated me to an exaggerated extent from the place I'd grown up in. From my Wattville Road class of forty, only three of us went to the Boys' Grammar School and two or three to the Girls'. Nobody from Kentish Road had ever gone before, except my own sister and brother, years before. This fact, the expectation that all the Fisher children were on the conveyor belt and in the process of being educated out of the street, set the family apart, in an odd way. We weren't brash or go-getting, but there was a slight air of our having received a higher call.

Handsworth Grammar School was a nineteenth-century foundation. Like nearly all such places it had developed the function of educating the sons of local lower-middle-class families—technical, clerical, shopkeeping, the sort of people who didn't send their children away to boarding schools—to perpetuate that class, and in addition to draw promising working-class boys "up" into it. The handful of us from Wattville Road were of the latter sort; certain other schools in better-off neighbourhoods sent their boys to the grammar school *en masse*. The staff was fairly typical, except for its Head, a product of public school and Cambridge, a haughty, cold-mannered zealot, an Anglican cleric and a Buchmanite, whose declared aim was to reproduce, as far as was possible in such a place, the ethos of a public school like Arnold's Rugby. Its application was to be local, to feed industry with technically and scientifically trained personnel, in the process declassing any whose class origins were likely to hamper their social mobility. We were encouraged, for instance, to lose the local characteristics in our speech; with the blood of servants running in my veins, and some talent for mimicry, I turned out to be quite good at this game. The family accent wasn't a strongly-marked Brummagem, but tended to take on different characteristics according to the occupations its speakers followed. I easily acquired a neutral, go-anywhere accent—so easily that I later felt angry at the way it had smoothed out of my memory the speech I first had. I can't hear my own voice.

I soon learned that painting played no part in the school's plans for my advancement. The top stream into which I was put had no art in its curriculum, no examinable music, no geography or history. I let my painting and drawing go without a fight; I couldn't see what the fight could have been. I kept them going as private activities for a while, but the talent didn't survive puberty. By this time, though, I was singing, untrained, in the school choir, having taken to it too late to make the sort of mark my father and brother—who had followed him as head chorister at Saint Mary's, as did my son Joe—had made. Technically I did join that choir, conquering my distaste for the liturgy and the fancy dress, but so late that during a bout of pneumonia that came between my audition and my debut my voice had broken. But it was to be music that first replaced painting for me.

That illness, a couple of months away from the world after passing through mortal danger, was a rite of passage, a *Magic Mountain* in miniature. I spent most of it in my room, looking out at the sky over the factory yard and the field, watching the spring arrive, reading, drawing, and thinking. My feelings sharpened and clarified. After the confusion and pain of the illness had passed, I was happy in my isolation. I experienced, in fact, many of the sensations of Mann's hero. I was twelve. When I emerged, I was less of a child.

I hadn't become a conventional, active adolescent; I lurked behind a vaguely juvenile manner for years. But it was as if I'd been somewhere unknown, and had come back altered. Wherever it was, it's the location of my imagination; it's still the place I have to find in order to write, and its essential qualities never alter. It combines a sense of lyrical remoteness with an apprehension of something turbulent, bulky, and dark. There, I don't have to bother to grow older.

I didn't move towards writing at that time, though I was reading everything I could find—and also listening to the radio. We'd acquired a radio only a little while before the war began, and I spent, like almost everybody else, a great part of the next five years listening to BBC broadcasts indiscriminately. The BBC was still very much as Reith had left it; it was also wartime, and the British, disoriented, had inadvertently dropped some of their defences against experiencing the arts. It was from reading the *Radio Times*, in those days an earnest and responsible journal, that I first realised there was an adult world of music, painting, and writing all around me, out of immediate reach but capable of being sought after. Very gradually, I found my way around. It was late in 1943, when I had the musical tastes of an unassisted thirteen-year-old—I knew all the popular tunes of the day, along with a little Handel, a little Rossini, Tchaikovsky, Holst, Grieg—that I was knocked permanently into a different trajectory by a single record heard on a request programme. This was Meade Lux Lewis's 1936 piano solo, "Honky Tonk Train Blues." In the three minutes it took to hear it, it seemed as if every cell I had was mobilised to go in search of those unimagined sounds, which seemed to have nothing to do with any music I'd ever heard—even jazz, which had simply sounded rackety, overurgent stuff.

In those same minutes, I realised that my new passion was to be yet another of my secrets: nobody would approve of it. I began listening to any programmes where the music might appear, dissembling my intense interest, even joining in the insults it provoked when it showed up. I started scraping away at our semiderelict piano in an attempt to reproduce what I was hearing, and kept on doing so until I had some success, believing all the while that my ambition was secret. I don't know how I persuaded myself that this could be. The noise, in a small house, was loud, brutal, and insistent; neighbouring shift-workers complained. My parents suggested I should take lessons, probably in the hope that my practice would become more euphonious, but I declined, believing that the lessons would come between me and what I wanted to play – and, by declining, storing up years of technical troubles; I was to reach fifty before I took any lessons.

It wasn't long before my pursuit of piano boogie opened up the whole of jazz. I listened to whatever was broadcast—we had no gramophone—and, almost more important, read whatever there was to read. Two books, Wilder Hobson's *American Jazz Music* and Hugues Panassié's *Le Jazz hot* modelled as they were on orthodox musical criticism and intent on assimilating the new art to the traditional ones, were the first developed writings about any of the arts I ever encountered. I read them over and over again, and can still call whole sentences up from memory. They had an enormous influence on the way I thought in general, and in particular, directed my taste to a congenial quarter, the white Chicago musicians who came up in the twenties and continued to work in association with Eddie Condon—Bud Freeman, Dave Tough, Joe Sullivan, Pee Wee Russell, Jess Stacy. Of all the men who had ever made jazz, these constituted the only group whose circumstances were at all like my own.

The passion for jazz and for the piano was one of the positive lurches. It kept me going through a dreary period of school examinations, and the last stages of the war and its aftermath. By the end of 1943 I'd grown out of feeding off the war in any way, and it had turned to an endless dull horror. I was not cheered by the atomic bomb, or by the manifest state of things as the Cold War set in. My father's brief prosperity ended, and he went back, none too happily, to his jewellery firm. The young men of the family came back, much older and without illusions. At school, I moved up into the vestigial Arts Sixth, without objectives and feeling much further out of my depth than I need have done. There was an undertow of what I can only describe as unfelt sadness, somehow drawing my spirits down, not dramatically but gently and steadily.

Sometime early in 1946 I left the world, and stayed away from it for three years. Afterwards, I found it hard to get back, and I still sometimes experience the recurring shadow of that time. What happened was that I radically revalued the currency of my dealings with my life: I renegotiated my contract. In the quiet madness that took hold of me I became convinced, without any evidence, that I had an unknown, virtually undetectable form of tuberculosis, and was already too far gone for treatment to be of any use. I had two or three years left at the most. I would certainly never see twenty. More to the point, I would never have to.

The disease was then still a common-enough killer of young people, and I'd seen it at work; and I imagine my particular form of hysteria is common enough in the literature—though the only person I've ever known who entertained it, and in an almost identical form, is another poet, Patricia Beer. At all events, I now held the biggest of all my secrets. I was dead. No one must know. The shock would kill my parents, naturally; so delay their learning about it as long as possible. As the possessor of a deadly disease, I also had the power of life and death over everybody I met. I had no inclination to be other than merciful, so for three years I didn't, apart from the odd unavoidable handshake and an arm's-length dandling of my newborn nieces, touch another human being. This was easy. Nobody observed any change in my behaviour, and there probably was none.

I was extremely healthy. In order to guard my secret I didn't go near a doctor for the whole of the period, nor did I need to. I stayed fat, cycled everywhere—while I could, until the unmistakable signs should appear. I kept on reading, coasted through schoolwork, developed my piano playing to the point where I could start appearing in public, sitting in with a band and playing solo spots at local jazz clubs.

Everything, though, was temporary. I put down nothing for the future, prepared nothing, confided in nobody. The renegotiated contract meant that I needed to do nothing beyond dabbling, diverting myself from my awful fate. As for motivation and structure, they were taken care of by the daily business of preserving my cover—for I wanted to remain at large as long as I could get away with it, secure in the knowledge that it wouldn't be for an inconveniently long time. I'd had almost enough of life: I didn't want in, but I didn't want out strongly enough to commit suicide. Indeed, I didn't have the strength of feeling of a suicide.

I structured my life as a spy must—days of low-key activities, offbeat, bitchy humour, casual-seeming appearances here and there, all within the main concern of preserving cover. I did enough work, for instance, to get myself a university place (whatever that might be—I didn't know) simply because attending a university would delay the army medical which would expose me and consign me precipitately to the sanatorium where I would spend my last months in the composition of a few important poems, probably in the style of Matthew Arnold. When I learned that Birmingham University, where my place was, administered a medical to all freshmen, I stayed at school for a further year to try for a scholarship at Cambridge, which, so far as I knew, didn't do anything so intrusive. That step meant that I was made Head Prefect, a position of greater power than any I've held since. I was a quite efficient disciplinary bureaucrat, operating with the arrogance the job traditionally demanded and with an added quiet menace generated by my understandably distant attitude to the whole thing. It was splendid cover. On one occasion I even evaded a compulsory mass chest X-ray call by marshalling the entire school, boys and masters, onto the buses that took them to the radiography centre, then omitting to join the trip myself.

I didn't get the Cambridge scholarship. My motivation was too oblique, and my preparation hopelessly inadequate; the school wasn't equipped for such work. I had to fall back on Birmingham and its medical, and make the most of the months that remained. When I left school my remote and disaffected manner earned me a beta-plus for Personality in place of the customary straight A awarded to Head Prefects. It was an unprecedented snub. I thought it no bad score, for a corpse.

Going to the university changed my spectral life hardly at all. I cycled a couple of miles beyond the school each day, to the old Arts Faculty building in the city centre. I didn't know at first what course my school had enrolled me for. It didn't matter. I didn't buy books; I made notes in the backs of old school exercise books. I got caught up in a student jazz band, and decided to stay alive until its November Carnival gig; my medical would probably not fall due till February or March.

But the call came early. I cycled halfway to the medical centre, hallucinated chest pains, and phoned in my excuses. I was told to see my own doctor. He told me I had flu, completely failing to observe the wrecked condition of my lungs. Nobody at the postponed medical spotted anything either. The chest X-ray I had would show it all, though. Waiting for the recall, I heard of other students being called in for repeats. But no message came for me. My game was up and I had to recognise it. I was alive, and must immediately adjust to the fact. Instantly and completely, I forgot the delusion which had dominated my life for three years. I mentioned it to nobody, and didn't remember it for a further two years. It was only then that I understood how mad I'd been, and it was the forgetting I found more frightening than the delusion itself.

After that moment in my nineteenth year, I had to begin my life, at the point to which my long absence had let it drift. I had to learn—and quickly— to study, smoke, drink, dance, compete, talk to girls, get around generally. At first I worked frantically to catch up lost ground, with the simple aim of not getting thrown out of the university. I overshot and did rather well, made friends, got around. The local jazz scene of which I'd been a part for a year or two was in a trough, and there was less in it for me. While I was still at death's door I'd played solo at a big concert (insisting, in the interests of secrecy, that my name be excluded from all publicity) and had been invited to make a record for review in the leading jazz magazine—which I did. But the game was turning sour; maybe I realised that in my years away I'd equipped myself, technically, only very poorly and wasn't going to be able to sustain the chances that were coming my way. I broke engagements abruptly, and gave up playing in public for quite a few years.

I came to feel, as I turned nineteen, that I ought to want to write. I seemed to be becoming the sort of young man who had that wish. Thomas Mann's *Doktor Faustus*, which I first read about this time, had a good deal to do with it; my recent experience qualified me to be sceptical about its thesis, but the account of Leverkühn's artistic education made deliberate creative work seem possible. The insights linked up with something that had happened three years before, at the very onset of my imaginary malady, but which had had to remain isolated and dormant. The school sent a party of us to a belated piece of wartime cultural education. For the time it was something unheard of: a three-day course in film education. Fine gentlemen—Charles Frend, Michael Balcon, Roger Manvell—lectured us about their close experience of this art, and had us sitting goggling at films the like of which we'd never seen before: *Metropolis, Alexander Nevsky, The Plow That Broke the Plains, Night Mail, Steel, Drifters.* There was nothing academic about it all. It just hit hard. Again, there was a disruptive sense of what was possible. I don't think it strange that *Doktor Faustus* didn't make me want to be a composer, just as the film course didn't make me want to direct films; I've grown used to having poetic ideas opened up by arts other than poetry.

Gradually, I got the idea of writing into focus, chiefly by reading, wave on wave of whatever contemporary or recent work I could get hold of, altering taste and orientation by the week. In September 1949, I began keeping an intense, precious journal of my sensibility, and within a month had arrived at a poem. It was meant as a pledge of allegiance to early Dylan Thomas, and every word of it was false, but to be able to write it at all gave me a sense of exultant power. Naturally, I kept the whole thing to myself. I wrote more: pastiches of Auden, Empson, Henry Reed, in rapid succession. Writing was very difficult. I had a certain ability at phrase-making, but no facility of thought or form at all. I was working against resistances quite as formidable as the manual and theoretical problems posed by the piano keyboard.

After nearly a year, my reading had taken me to a stage where I could understand poetry as going beyond verbal sensations to a way of analysing cultures, and I wrote, in some excitement and with much more assurance, a short dramatic monologue in pentameters. The speaker was a King Lear analogue, and he spoke severally through the mouths of Yeats, Rilke, Eliot, and Rafael Alberti—and probably more. There were a few poets around the university: R. F. Willetts was teaching Greek, D. J. Enright was an extramural tutor, and Paul West, not yet a novelist, was a final-year undergraduate. They often attended a staff-student writers' group. I read my piece there, and got plenty of encouragement. The university magazine published it; a door of sorts was opening.

I graduated, well enough to be given a research scholarship, and proceeded to go quietly to pieces again. I'd been good at quick, impressionistic criticism, but didn't know how to work systematically. I was setting out to solve some of the conundrums of metrical analysis, but was too full of a sort of libertarian dogmatism to get anywhere with it. I'd been running with a pack of Jungians and reading Robert Graves; my mind was animated but hardly open. I was obsessed with patterns and hierarchies. My poems became flat, dogmatic arrangements of symbols; my imagination was a panhistoric costume drama.

In an act which seems to me far more bizarre than my imaginary illness, but of which I'm more ashamed, since it was real, I joined a Christian church, on an intellectual whim. I decided that the cult of the Great Mother was magically perpetuated in the sacraments of the Christian church, and that I needed to receive those sacraments in order to share that magical linkage. The ultimate aim would be to subvert the Christian churches back into the Old Religion. I positioned myself at the highest, most ritualistic point of Anglo-Catholicism I could find, took the sacraments, and acquired a pious religiosity, while keeping my real intentions from my instructors. All this was most perverse, for I've always had a deep repugnance for Christianity, in its essence, and for its role in history—an attitude similar to that of Edward Gibbon, and held for similar reasons. But unaccustomed to action or commitment, I was forcing myself against my own nature—was, in fact, forcing my nature to abdicate and submit to something alien and uncongenial.

This went on for a year or two, fading slowly. It wasn't a good period. My scholarship wasn't renewed, for my intellect was being seriously disabled by its own efforts, and by my naïve flailing around for something—preferably something stuffy—to believe in. I'd edited the university magazine, but had run out of steam early and relinquished the editorship. I was still living with my parents, but was withdrawn into my own preoccupations, and oppressed by their many troubles; I was drawn to try to help them, but felt powerless. They were now in their sixties and seeming older. My father's health was breaking down by way of a series of strokes; he was often very anxious, and the damage to his brain brought his thinking and talk down into a more and more limited compass.

In my last year at the university I tried to continue my research while training as a teacher. It wasn't a career I wanted to follow, but I had no other plans, and it was the only job I'd ever watched anyone else doing extensively. Occasionally I wrote doctrinaire fantasy poems, but published only a few of them, I socialised a good deal; my friend Barbara Venables and I spent most of our time at the theatre or in pubs, dressing up and laying the law down. We got married while we were still both students. We were married for many years, and had two sons, Joe and Ben; we stayed friends through that, and remain so now.

My working life started in a characteristically ghostly fashion. When my student exemption from military service ran out, a couple of minor disabilities caused me to be declared unfit, but only on a temporary basis; I could be called in again at any time. The medical exemption was acceptable, for it saved me the trouble of going through the charade of disguising my political objections to military service as reservations of a more tender sort, and still paying a social penalty; but its temporary nature left me in a limbo of an all-too-familiar kind. I could only take a job under false pretences. Which I proceeded to do. I became a teacher at a grammar school in Newton Abbot, in Devon, expecting to be called away at any time, and for that reason living from day to day and putting down no roots. There was no way I could resolve my situation, and instead I treated it as unreal, even to the extent of concealing my address from the authorities and ignoring official summonses when they reached me. Again it was a life of temporary experiences, temporary sensations. It was over a year before an inescapable call caught up with me. This time I failed the medical conclusively. Once again I had to accept my situation as real, and catch up with it.

We lived in Torquay at first, in a squalid, rickety flat, and later in more comfort in Newton Abbot, and I found the area fascinating—for its towns more than its countryside: I'd never lived away from Birmingham before. I'd had no wish to become a schoolteacher; and it was perhaps this lack of seriousness and method which made me turn out to be, from my point of view, disconcertingly good at it. I hated schools as institutions as much as I had done as a pupil, so I treated it all as a compulsory game, and took risks I wouldn't have taken as a serious professional. I read Homer Lane and A.S. Neill, and taught accordingly. The results, of course, were pretty good. Although I didn't enjoy being a teacher, this experience, over the four years I spent there, taught me more about living in the real world than did all my explorations of the West Country. Those gave me enormous pleasure, but they contributed only to my increasingly tortuous fantasy life, which started, in about 1954, to break out into poems again. It was about that time that I came across the work of John Cowper Powys; different from me in almost every imaginable way, he was nevertheless able to show me how to accept an obsessional, quite unpresentable inner existence, a private madness, as a life force to be harnessed rather than locked in and ignored. For a while I worked more in the hope of producing massive novels like his than of making poems. Such poems as I did write were bulky and suffused, or manic, completely dedicated to psychic self-exploration. I'd grown out of the cold ritualism of a few years before, but there was nothing in my poems that might interest anybody else, except a certain energy and a perverse rhetorical force.

It was that odd energy which got me into publication and into touch with what has turned out to be my work. In 1954 a couple of my shorter fantasy poems were broadcast in a local radio programme run by Charles Causley, and some time later John Sankey took one for his nonconformist little magazine, *The Window*. I thought nothing of this, I'd been paid seven-and-sixpence, on condition that I let Sankey alter one line, and had grown out of the poem anyway; but I was surprised to receive a letter from one of the other contributors, Gael Turnbull, whose (as it seemed to me then) perilously slight, purist lyrics I'd noticed. He'd been commissioned to furnish a selection of new British poetry for an issue of Cid Corman's *Origin*, then still in its first series, and, importantly, close to the most vital initiatives in the poetry of Black Mountain College. The mandate was to find British poets who were outside the orthodoxy of the time. I was no Black Mountain poet; I was just another muffled English provincial eccentric. But I was certainly well outside the neat, socially-oriented orthodox poetic, which had neither appeal nor meaning for me. I couldn't even mimic it.

Gael Turnbull, part Scot, part Swede, educated in England and the United States, and just returned from a spell in Canada to work in a London hospital before settling in Worcester, was another inevitable outsider; we had that much in common. Apart from the entrée to *Origin*—Corman approved of what I was doing and used three of my more lightly constructed fantasy pieces—he was able to show me a great deal. On a two-day visit to Worcester late in 1956, I saw for the first time the work of the later Williams, Basil Bunting, Robert Duncan, Alan Ginsberg, Louis Zukofsky, Irving Layton, Robert Creeley, Lawrence Ferlinghetti, Denise Levertov, Charles Tomlinson, Larry Eigner, and Charles Olson. I'd never seen poetry used as these people were, in their various ways, using it, nor had I seen it treated as so vital an activity. These people were behaving with all the freedom and artistic optimism of painters. Decidedly un-English.

I went home and tackled my writing from a new direction. I had already on occasion used chance operations to begin poems I didn't think important; now I used such methods extensively—usually short phrases picked at random, often by my wife, Barbara, who would sometimes arrive at them by automatic writing. The main effect of the method was to get me out of my own way. This was very necessary. I'd grown up with no trace of the compact self which most other people seemed to have; instead I had a diffused zone in which ad hoc selves would be generated for temporary purposes, and then dissolve again. Establishing a usable, consistent self was later to prove a lengthy business, like growing a windbreak. The self I'd tried in those days to fix as a writing *persona* was just a kind of self-important bruise, a posture. It got in the way, and didn't ring true. Once rid of it, though, I could get at observations, memories, earlier selves, lost feelings, casual things—reality, in short—and my clotted language cleared like a cloudy liquid left to settle. Almost immediately a poem called "Midlanders" turned up; it didn't quite succeed, but it showed me for the first time that I had material close to hand, from my own experience, and access to an unforced way of handling it. Although by my earlier standards my new poems were oblique, casual, and obscure, people started reading them and publishing them. Before long I was in receipt of postal tutorials from Cid Corman and correspondence from Denise Levertov, Larry Eigner, and the British poets and editors Robert Cooper and Bill Price Turner. I was out when Louis and Celia Zukofsky called at our flat in Newton Abbot; but they called, nevertheless.

Gael Turnbull was, in the years that followed, single-handedly responsible for whatever currency I had as a poet. I'd send bundles of work off to him as I wrote it. He was in touch with many editors, and would quietly place my work in magazines I'd not even heard of. I seldom tried pushing my work even then, having a gift for choosing the wrong ones. Soon I gave up, and left nature to take its course; for twenty or thirty years I've been able to rely on invitations—partly since I write relatively little.

I was in a liberated mood, too, because I had, or thought I had, the prospect of giving up full-time teaching. I was being given advancement at the school, and that made me uncomfortable, for I was thereby losing my position as a licensed young experimenter and being brought into the hierarchy. In a year or two I'd be in charge of a department, then in line for a headship, which would involve my identifying myself, to a greater extent than I was willing to do, with the generally Christian and conservative ethos of schools of that sort—indeed, most schools. We decided to go back to Birmingham. Barbara would teach—in Devon I'd had the only job for which we were both qualified—while I'd work part-time in a primary school, and, for the rest, build up a connection as a piano player. As it turned out, her teaching job turned into our son Joe, and I had to hang on to a full-time post in a school so hellishly unruly that I resigned before my year was out, with no job to go to.

Luck, and my teaching testimonials, landed me comfortably on my feet in a college of education, in one of the Black Country towns on the western edge of Birmingham. The place was run on breathtakingly hypocritical and paternalist lines, and my political education was considerably advanced; what I learned, I endeavoured to pass on to my students. But the duties were pleasant, and I was more effective as a teacher of teachers than of children directly. The pay was poor, though, and the penury I'd experienced ever since I went onto a payroll was deepening with a family to keep, so I needed all the piano-playing work I could get. We lived for the next thirteen years back in Handsworth, in a house we couldn't at first afford, a few hundred yards from my mother's old home, Ivy Cottage, by then embedded in a housing estate. For the first five of those years I was constantly out at nights, playing in Dixieland bands, bebop quartets, and Black Country dance bands; for a while I was the token white in the Andy Hamilton Caribbean Combo. I played in jazz clubs, town halls, village halls, strip clubs, dance halls, drinking clubs, and hotels. There was still plenty wrong with my playing, but I got by, and enjoyed it. It was a belated version of my surrendered adolescence.

Living in constant, and apparently inescapable debt darkened my spirits to some extent, and I wrote poetry less freely. But I found that returning to Birmingham after an absence had given me an artist's distance from it. I wanted to write about it, and became immersed in its associative power. My journeys through it in connection with my educational work and my piano playing were in all directions at all hours of the day and night. I saw it from the oddest of angles. Without any particular aim I started on the voluminous series of prose pieces and poems which I was to help Michael Shayer to edit down to the Migrant pamphlet *City* which appeared, as my first collection, in 1961.

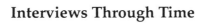

Interviews Through Time

Beginnings

John Tranter: Let's look at the matter of poetic development. Where did you begin as a writer when you first decided you wanted to write poetry rather than prose, or make movies or whatever else you might have wanted to do? And where did you learn to write from? Did you learn to write from English models, or from models in other languages?

Roy Fisher: I started at the age of nineteen, from the first place I could find anything which I thought crudely exciting enough to break the rather grey surface of my mind. I knew there was something that I wanted to make. I didn't know what it was. All I'd studied up to that stage, and had felt any sympathy with was a sort of statuesque nineteenth-century diction. Matthew Arnold was my idea of sensible development from the heady stuff like Keats. Had I started writing in that mood, all would have been lost, I think. But I knew better than that, and was completely stuck, and literally had—it may be a very common experience—a feeling of something wanting to be made, but not telling me at all what it was. I got in through reading surrealist or neo-surrealist texts, things like Salvador Dali's autobiography, or Dylan Thomas' prose works.

    The first poem I wrote, when I was nineteen, was a cheap trip through Dylan Thomas' stage properties. Nobody who's read me in print since would believe that. I still own the poem somewhere. I've never revealed it to anybody. I started in from steam heat, by raising the temperature and melting the language, and writing a lingo that never was. I went very far from conversation. I don't think I was very conversational at that stage. So I wrote in a special fine language and continued to do that, getting a bit more educated in what I did along the way. I remember writing the first thing I published—it was in a student magazine—it was a sort of *King Lear* dramatic monologue, where the old man is going out in a rather quiet way to die, and in the forty or fifty lines of this monologue he not only copies certain writers but he also alludes to them by quotation: Eliot, Yeats, Lorca, Rilke, Rafael Alberti, it was quite a catalogue. I went through the book, you know, being very eclectic indeed.

JT: I think Eliot said that poets learn to write by being other writers for a while, and then moving on to another one.

RF: I was being all of them, at that period. Then I went on, I got more of a smell of what the hard stuff was like. Oddly enough, from Robert Graves, who was surfacing, again, about this time. He was having one of his periods of being interesting. This was the early fifties. *The White Goddess* had come out and that interested me very much. Too much, at the time. I was interested in the really very tough but committedly imaginative strain that there is in Graves. You know, there is part of his poetry where he really means business, and I was interested in the not very decorated style of writing that he had, the style that was very close to a brusque off-hand conversational style. I learnt some things from that.

RF: I started writing when I was about twenty, and I wrote some student poetry. I had no contacts at all, nor did I for a long time afterwards; and then I started doodling again when I was about 24 or 25 in an utterly, classically corny thing, and listening to one of those local radio things on what is now Radio 4, *West Country Poets*; I was working in Devon. It was a sort of situation where you're utterly short of five quid and your wife says: 'Good God, you could do that'. So I wrote sort of imitative, *Poetry Review*—1950's period *Poetry Review*! —poetry under a pseudonym. I actually wrote a con poem pretending to be by a retired brigadier; it was semi-automatic too (my wife was doing automatic writing and I was just picking words out). And I wrote some sonnets which were the sort of thing a retired military man of sensitivity might write about the view in the Middle East, a place where I had never been. I sent them up to Charles Causley who ran the programme, and I had a note back saying: 'these are very promising, but I don't think they quite come off. Please send some more'. So I then sent some of my own things which were not terrific poems in any way, but they were technically interesting, and they broadcast a few of them, and from then on I felt that I existed a bit and I could pay the gas bill out of these tiny bits of money the BBC paid. But in terms of what one knew at that point, I was reading anything but what would make an O.K. poetry. I had read some poems—but that was late—I had read some Wallace Stevens; I had not read any Williams; I had not known what was going on; I had a thoroughly heterogeneous non-O.K. taste because I had no contacts. I was reading Rilke, I was reading Stefan George, Apollinaire, anything that came up, but I was not in touch with anybody else who was writing at all, and consequently had no programme. After that, by one or two quite tenuous things, I had a poem, a very late romantic poem, in a little magazine called *The Window* which John Sankey was running; Gael Turnbull saw it and for some reason—his ostensible reason was that it reminded him of Irving Layton—recruited me for *Origin*. That brought me immediately into the barrage of Cid Corman's correspondence and that, at the age of 26 or 27, I started to teach me something about the actual language and the recent history of poetry. Again, to be historical, whereas I could turn out a poem which was not committed in any particular direction and George Macbeth would broadcast it; and when I was appearing in Black Mountain spin-off publications and achieved a bit of an identity in that, the English establishment of the time did not want to know.

JT: What about the influence of the English 'Movement' poets of the fifties, did you ever feel drawn to want to write in that style at all?

RF: No, I couldn't even mimic it. I can do imitations of things but I couldn't understand enough of what made those people tick, even to send them up.

JT: What about Larkin? Larkin was one of them but his writing style is very impressive, even to a young writer, I'd think. Even if you don't like it, you have to respond to it.

RF: Yes, I had a sort of near brush with Larkin. Larkin was about eight years older than I am. It was the point where I started having some currency, the things I've been talking about happened when I was a student around the early 1950s. I then stopped, and purely by this sort of chance that happens to people who are just sitting in their bed sitting rooms wondering what to do in their nights off, I wrote one or two little pieces without any content to them, without any meaning. They were little decorative fantasy pieces, and I sent one off to local radio station. It got broadcast. Then I had a thing in a magazine called *The Window*, which was a not very establishment-minded little magazine, John Sankey ran it. Whereas the Movement people were coming through things like *Encounter* and *The London Magazine*, they were hitting the mainstream, and if you weren't that, you weren't going to get in. And Gael Turnbull saw it in *The Window*—he's a person of very mixed background and a congenital outsider—he was collecting material for a guest-edited number of Cid Corman's magazine *Origin*, the first series. And he was completely free in what he chose. Gael was temperamentally not interested in the English mainstream so he went sniffing around the outside.

One of the people he chose to be in this issue of Corman's magazine, along with me, was Larkin, who seemed to him not typical of the English and also obviously very good. I think at that stage the full biliousness of Larkin's outlook on life hadn't come through in the verse, and Larkin was not a man who was making pronouncements about the century having moved on too fast. He hadn't cultivated his Eeyore qualities, the persona he developed in middle life. Larkin was sent a complimentary copy of the magazine, to see what kind of magazine he was going to be in. He opened it and—I don't know whether it was the impact of what he read, or the fact that his book was coming out shortly—he sent by registered post a countermand to withdraw all his material. So he wasn't published along with Irving Layton and Charles Olson and Larry Eigner and untidy people like that. But our paths were close together for a little while there.

JT: That must have been an interesting moment in English literary history. If only one could have realised what the past and the future would have looked like in fifty years time...

RF: Well, if he'd been in the magazine, I don't think that sort of thing would have stuck with him. He wasn't interested in opening the experience out.

I found it a very windswept world of the mind to get involved with that, and to find that suddenly I was getting correspondence course lessons from Cid Corman. He was telling me what was happening in Black Mountain. This was the mid-fifties. It was a completely new world. And as an ordinary crusty young Englishman I found it new. I went some way along with it, but I wasn't ready to run with it all the way.

JT: So you read the American writers but at a bit of a distance, and it was a distance you wanted to keep. Was that because of where you were born?

RF: I'm a Midlander, which is a very particular sort of race. It's supposed to be nowhere at all. I haven't got the near-nationalism which Basil Bunting has. He had himself referred to as a 'Northumbrian', because Northumbria was an old kingdom, and its language is descended slightly differently [from other kinds of English] and its political institutions and its exposure to invaders from Scandinavia, and the way it was treated by the Norman French invaders; all this gave it a different fate from the body of England. I'm a Mercian, if Bunting was a Northumbrian. I come from the no-account bit in the middle.

I'm—because of what in England we call 'social class'—I come from the thing called the 'working class', and I didn't go to one of the older universities, and I've never lived in London. I'm a provincial. Someone in a review said 'Fisher's subject matter is, I suppose, always "the provinces"'. Which is everywhere else but London and Oxford and Cambridge, and one or two rather well-to-do spots around that way. It doesn't mean much, but it affects the way you behave, and what you root for and what you snarl at.

JT: It also helps to determine where you appear in print, doesn't it?

RF: It can do. One mustn't caricature, and certainly the people I think of as being on Establishment railway lines will fight back indignantly if you imply that certain ways are open to certain people and closed to others. But I think it certainly happened in my generation that ... it's quite easy to be invisible. I don't mind being invisible if it gives me independence. But there were times when you could feel more invisible than you wanted to be, simply because of the very strongly metropolitan habits that England has. There's the 'express route' through into anything to do with the media of print and broadcasting. There are exceptions. But traditionally it would go from a 'public' (i.e. a private) school, it would go very commonly to Oxford, it would go into London. And the habit of starting a magazine, the habit of being in contact with people who are published, the people who have access to radio and so forth, it comes rather quickly, and there's a network of passing favours and getting things done. Which means that people can be on their feet and up and running in their early twenties. And that happens to a lot of people.

JT: Some of them are aware of it. I was reading a recent autobiographical piece by Thom Gunn. He said he left England and went to America partly because of how easy it was, he saw, for him and his friends to get into print in London. He went to Cambridge, and he said he went down to London, and he found it very easy to get reviewed well by his friends. For him I don't think there was any point in any of that at all, because it didn't have anything to do with what you were worth as a writer.

RF: He's a good guy from that point of view. The carry on of that quick burst into celebrity that Thom Gunn had, it lasted him for twenty, twenty-five years in this country. He'd come back for a reading—I met him at a reading full of parties of school kids, and he was surprised. He says no one pays this much attention to him in the United States, what's it all about? It was the momentum. I remember picking up the *London Magazine* in my early twenties, and saying 'Who's this new poet? He's got a come-on. He's got a style.' And there he was, bam bam. Ted Hughes the same. It's not to be sneezed at. Whether that road through into publication affected the way people put things down, whether it makes them less shaggy, uncouth or odd—I wouldn't call Ted Hughes other than shaggy, uncouth and odd, in his early days, and his Yorkshire-ism is very strong—but at the same time it may give you an idea of know-how about what it is to write a publishable text. Just as if someone said to you at an early age 'Come and help me make this movie—hold this'—you'll know something about making a movie, other than you would know if you sat in a pub for fifteen years saying 'It's going to be a great movie, I can see it all in my mind's eye,' and you'd never been on a set. I think there are things like that, that work. And this has not got much to do with poetry, as poetry, but it may have something to do with the medium in which poetry exists.

The Sixties: from *City* to *Matrix*

Eric Mottram:How did *City* come to be published in *Living Arts* in 1963, then?

RF: Either John Bodley, who was a reader, or Theo Crosby, who was an architect, nicked it up and was interested, either by something in its literary properties, or because it talked a great deal about bricks and mortar and streets and townscape.

EM: Something that fitted the programme of the magazine.

RF: It appealed accidentally.

EM: Did you submit *City* to *Kulchur* magazine or did they invite you to?

RF: No, I suddenly found it was there. I had never heard of *Kulchur* magazine. What I used to do—a picture of an enormously passive career is building up—what happened was that Gael Turnbull was in California and I would automatically type stuff up and send it to him and was in touch by letter a great deal; I would just routinely send stuff, and he was fully into, as I was only partly, the extremely widespread and active correspondence which was going among the alumni of Black Mountain College and some people they had picked up by the way, for five or six years afterwards. People like Lita Hornick who was running *Kulchur* magazine, would say, 'Have you anything interesting in your bag?', and Gael was one of these people who had work to send out. Indeed, I didn't hustle any of this work, but I was constantly finding work had been taken, and strange things would happen such as: very shortly after I had heard of any of these people at all, I got home from school in Devon one afternoon and my wife said there was a man called Louis Zukofsky who had been here all afternoon, with his little boy and his wife and a cellist who stood on his head on the mat, and he didn't know who you were—as well he might not have: I'd published nothing and I had only had a quick glance at something of Zukofsky's. I might have found conversation very difficult but my wife had entertained him by telling him how she thought he should pronounce the name 'Eliot', whom he was on his way to see, and his chief interest had been whether he should address him as 'Mr Elliott', or 'Mr Elyot'. That sort of thing would happen through this network. The idea of this stuff as we now have it, fed in rather hefty chunks in college situations, and published, is very different. I was one day writing to Cid Corman in Matera, and Jonathan Williams would show up on the doorstep with a camera another day; it was that sort of thing.

EM: What about Stuart Mills and *Tarasque*? At what point did he get interested in you? Did you contact him first, or, did he contact you?

RF: The astonishing thing about that is that he and I constitute an old boy network; we both went, some years apart to the same school, and it is not a school that anybody else ever went to, except a band leader called Jack Payne. This will infuriate all the other alumni of that school if they ever hear it said. But it so happened that Stuart Mills sent me, at some time or other, a load of stuff, city poetry, stretches of which, quite literally, I couldn't distinguish from my own writing. It wasn't imitative either, but we had lived in the same place and he was trained as a visual artist, which puts him somewhat on my side of things anyway. As a child, I was a graphic artist and painter, chiefly; I had very little to do with books; I still wouldn't call myself the bookish type. But Stuart must have picked up the city thing: in fact he was running a bookshop and he just started calling, visiting his mother-in-law in Birmingham.

EM: And then began to publish you?

RF: Yes.

EM: I think one of the best reviews appeared in *Tarasque*, by Stuart himself.

RF: Of *The Ship's Orchestra*. Yes, by Stuart and Simon Cutts, the co-editors.

EM: It was quite rare, at that time, to have an article at all, was it not? With all respect!

RF: Right. I think there were three reviews altogether of *The Ship's Orchestra*.

EM: One last group of questions, Roy, I would like to get to. I want to get to the use of metrics and the use of conventional prosodic methods. Do you remember how in a rash moment I recently asked you to write six hundred lines of iambic pentameters, since I wanted work for *Poetry Review*?

RF: And you got paid out didn't you?

EM: I got paid out, but it was partly a challenge, obviously, to get you going; but I would like to know what you think of the use of poetic conventions. Do you ever consider them?

RF: Yes

EM: If you do consider it, at what point do you say no, and what do you say yes to?

RF: This has occupied me a great deal because I am ... I have to pause and think this out because it is so important to me. If I am anything of any interest it is because I enjoy innovation and I can think best in a fairly radical position; the further I can take that, the better I work. At the same time, by temperament and upbringing and everything else, I am extremely hidebound or timid, if you like—I'll apply any word to it—slow off the mark, unwilling to let go all sorts of fruity and fulsome sides of literature, and I always want to find ways of taking some of the richer and more meaty sensations of writing or of the arts into more and more radical situations. Consequently, I find extreme formalism very appealing from the outside but quite hair-raising if I try to do it myself. Concrete, for instance, is for me dazzlingly right but physically quite beyond me. What happened, I think, in a lot of my writing, was that I was still trying— and this is partly to do with the sluggishness of my education, and slowness to start—the fact is, and I haven't mentioned this, but I would want to put it on the record, that I am very conscious, or have been very conscious, of things like class of origin, extreme provincialism, things of this sort; I am the opposite of metropolitan. And I was still struggling away, trying to get big effects in pentameters quite late in the day, and even after working in much freer forms, and much better, I think in the late fifties, was still going back and writing things like 'Five Morning Poems' (which are published in *Matrix* at last) which is in orthodox lines because I still wanted to get something out of those lines, or go round the back of Wallace Stevens and so forth. At the same time, I would never want to align myself with the kind of argument that still pops up about tension metrics and things of that sort. I don't want to engage in this. The only point of using any form is to create freedom forms and not to do things about impositions of order on chaos and that sort of rubbish.

But beyond that, what happened was that when I started writing, I found it difficult to write at all, to be an artist. This is a personal struggle—that I find it a great step, in my book, to commit a work of art, and one not to be taken lightly. There is a difficulty there, and also I can remember having a great sense of technical difficulty, in learning any techniques at all, to get from point to point. There came a time, I suppose around the early sixties, when I realised, somewhat to my surprise, that I could write whatever I could think; that verbally I had, in fact, a fair degree of fluency, and if I wanted to work up an impression of virtuosity—without making any comparisons—of the type, say, that Robert Duncan revels in like a great fish in the sea, I could work out some version of this kind of thing for myself which would show my faculties at large in a technical way. I then immediately clammed up and felt rather puritanical about it, and decided that that gave me a freedom to work in prose and to work in a much more taciturn fashion. I then decided that Wittgenstein's *Tractatus* was a very splendid sort of stylistic influence for one to adopt, and I paid far more attention to the *Tractatus* as a mode of lineation, say, than to any poet. And similarly, in more recent years, I have enjoyed the way Cage's thinking moves in his writing more than almost any poet.

EM: It is this that excites you, isn't it, that movement from one thing to the next, exploratively?

RF: Exactly. Linearity for me has very little to do with any of the things to do with breath or verse line and so forth; it has much more to do with the linearity of concepts, with the way in which ideas, mental experiences, line themselves, and can be taken through time sequences. I still stick a great deal to writing in linear sequences rather than doing things, which I know you have seen, where I work spatially out.

EM: That seemed to be important. You did one radical work I saw, and it was supposed to be part of a series; what happened to that?

RF: I did some more, and I found them in a sense easier to do and pleasant to do, but they were not carrying any of the sort of load of mental experience that I wanted them to carry, and I felt that there were probably other people who were graphically more gifted than I was who, could do that kind of thing better.

EM: Is the compositional procedure here, this linearity, a linear association procedure, and if so, do you check it afterwards?

RF: No.

EM: You let it stand.

RF: I let it stand, but sometimes cut. The ideal procedure for me, to date, over the work that I tend to like to stand by now, is to have an intensely realised starter, something which is more alive than I am, an idea that is more alive than I am, sitting there. This is why I have a block, probably.

EM: By 'idea', you would also mean a painting like the Monet waterlilies for 'Matrix'?

RF: No, it has to be something which is taken in, something that is within me, I'm talking of an insight which could be any stimulus you care to offer, nearly always take a chance stimulus. A lot of my poems are in fact chosen by pricking with a pin in a book of photographs and odd pictures, newspaper pictures and things. But the ideal procedure for me is to have an intensely realised starter and then I work something on the starter, and then I work the next thing on the things I've got so far. So the world is completely subsumed until the last moment of writing, and then I write further. *The Ship's Orchestra* is a model of this. I cheated or relaxed in some way; I wrote it particularly on certain paper that I had—I often do this—write inscriptions on certain paper, actual physical paper. And I then had a starter. I cheated insofar as I had certain revolving themes which I would feed in when the thing started to slow down so that I had numbers of little themes which kept coming round; but basically I would perfect every step and cut it and phrase it so that it would stand, and then I would write the next piece on the support of that, which meant that I could no longer alter what had gone before. So that I adopt, in fact, complete linearity of composition. The one thing I can't do is to sketch and to tidy up afterwards. I don't have a sense of a large overall form.

EM: That is, you feed into the automatic, as it were, a programmed action?

RF: Yes. It is a thing which Renoir used to do in his paintings, which was to try to have his painting at any moment in a state where it was balanced, so that if he stopped painting, he would have a picture. I like that.

EM: It is very like the abstract expressionists in America, too; at any given moment the thing is finished. But then you have got the problem that they all had, how do you know when to abandon it?

RF: You want to stop.

EM: Just that.

[Member of the Audience] When it's done.

RF: No, when *you're* done, when you have stopped doing the thing. You might want to go and do something else, or you might want to say, well, you've had enough of this. It gives you a very strange feeling when you read it, I mean, I have a job reading right through 'The Cut Pages', I'd rather shuffle it; I like it a few pages at a time. I constantly meet people who say—well, I don't constantly—but anybody I do meet who has had any time for *The Ship's Orchestra* will be like Gael Turnbull, who will merrily say: 'It's great, but I have never read it!'—never read it through, you know, because I'm simply not structuring things in any kind of way, with that kind of pay off. If they enjoy the feeling of, you know, fully grown babies' heads coming out of women's bodies, this is birth, this is what you are at, and this is what I like. That is the paradigm of the creation; you state a set of terms and you create further out of that set of terms. The thing you do not do is to refer out to an entailment in the outside world, you are breeding out of the work that you have demarcated as an art work. For me, the weight of the entailed world outside is extremely heavy and extremely imposing. One thing, maybe the last thing I can get in, about this block: in the early sixties: I used to find writing poetry relatively facile; it was not always good, but I felt, although I don't write a great deal, that I could always turn to a poem. But I had a massive ambition particularly —this is a very worthy piece of confession—but when you write poetry, it is nice to have some notice taken of it, and as you have said, I had very little notice indeed taken of what I did write. I didn't know how to push it or how to capitalise on what I had done, I am nobody's hustler, and I felt very little satisfaction or physical comeback for ten years' messing around, with poetry, and I very much wanted to write, I had a sort of ghost vision of a very massive novel, very massive prose form which I am in fact, by talent, the last person in the world to be able to write. I've still got notebooks, which occasionally I come across with astonishment, which are talking about characters which I, eight or nine years ago, seemed to know utterly everything about. It was like some Fellini film, written by Patrick White, something of this kind, or Herman Melville. It was a massive thing which has no reality in my mind at this moment but I was then trying to reach out, to heave up the sense of reality, in a Zolaesque sense almost, by sheer muscular force. I don't have that kind of force. I nearly knackered myself trying to generate it, where in fact my actual procedures are much more analytical.

EM: What did that mean when it said inside the front page, and also in Stuart Montgomery's blurb of *Collected Poems*, "the ghost of a paper bag"?

RF: I think that is part of the history of the book: what the book is, is a collection of poems I'd published or really a collection of pamphlets or other works. *City* is in there, for instance, 'Interiors' are there. I had first of all titled the collection *The Ghost of a Paper Bag* as being the expressive title. Over the time it took to assemble and publish it, which was, I suppose, about three years, I wasn't writing at all and didn't imagine that I was going to write again. The exigencies of publishing brought up a possibility of calling it *Collected Poems*, and since I thought it probably was my total work, I let it be called *Collected Poems*. Typographically, I wanted the title *The Ghost of a Paper Bag*, which was still how I thought of the book, ghosted in in grey, inside the book, but it got ghosted in in black on a page of its own, and it is still sort of drifting around there in the book. It looks like a motto but in actual fact it was the original title. It's always been reviewed as *Collected Poems*.

EM: In actual fact, too, in one of the advertisements, it is actually called *Collected Poems: Ghost of a Paper Bag*.

RF: I used to insist on that, but it got too long and I weakened.

EM: Why did you think you weren't going to write again? What was that about?

RF: Well, I had given up.

EM: Completely?

RF: Yes.

John Tranter: You mentioned in an earlier conversation that there was a period when you felt unable to write, then you broke out of that.

RF: I was a late starter. In my early and middle twenties I wrote in a very solitary fashion. It was very much to do with fantasy. I was pretty mad - in a quiet kind of way, but my head was filled with a very thick and lurid soup. And I wrote this thick and lurid soup. I wrote virtuoso pieces with metaphors dripping and trailing all over the place. Then almost by accident, in the middle of writing a lot of very decorative work, I found that I was making contact for the first time with people with a demanding aesthetic—and these were people like Creeley and Corman—whatever their aesthetic was, it was at least demanding. I met people like that for the first time, saw them at work. I didn't particularly want to follow the patterns they were working on. I certainly didn't want to follow the mannerisms. I often sat scribbling happily sending those mannerisms up. But I was impressed by finding anybody in literature talking with the sort of toughness that I knew very well that painters frequently talk with. Discussions of literary form among the 'Movement' people and their reviewers all seemed to me to be very stilted and petty, and far more to do with gang styles than to do with matters of making art, matters of composition. But here were these Americans who had been exposed to people like Albers and Buckminster Fuller; they were working to completely different rules from university literary fashion.

So then I got access to magazines. I'm very passive about this. If I'm asked to choose things, I learnt early on that I choose the wrong ones. So I thought, 'Let's see. Who wants what?' And Gael Turnbull was instrumental in getting me published at all. I would just send work to him as a friend. He knew everybody. He knew all the magazines, and was always feeding odd things into odd magazines. So I had quite a scattering of things published.

Then, again, things were taken almost out of my hands. Michael Shayer was the other partner with Gael Turnbull, and later, me, in the little international thing called Migrant Press, which bridged various things that were happening in America and in this country. Michael looked at my great heaving mass of odds and ends that I was writing about Birmingham, which was Rimbaud at one end, and, say, hard prose at the other, and saw that this material could be used as a kind of collage work; which he could see, and I couldn't. So he shook it around a bit and produced the first draft of *City* which was published in 1961 as a Migrant pamphlet. I didn't like it, but it caught people's attention. The knowledge that people were reading the stuff, and that it was not perfect, so far as I was concerned—it gave me a screaming fit. I could hardly move out of my chair for months. It really upset me.

I got used to it. I wrote various other things, slowly, then decided that this simply hadn't got enough leverage, it hadn't got enough power. I was learning to write the style I now write. But to be truthful, that had to be a fairly minimalist style, and I wanted more bulk or power. I spent ages trying to write a massive novel. Oddly enough, talking to an Australian, the person I had in mind was Patrick White, the way in which he could make great massive and epic effects. I was reading things like *Voss*, and being very impressed by large verbal structures, gothic or baroque things which would take you out of normality.

So ... I did that, and spent a lot of energy on it for a year or two, and got two or three sentences written, and a lot of notebooks. And I thought to hell with this, this is not succeeding, I'll go back to poetry. And when I went back to it, the poetry wasn't there. And so ...

JT: ... Oh dear.

RF: ... I was on the rocks. I was on the rocks for years. I couldn't write at all.

In the middle of this period I met Stuart Montgomery who was setting up Fulcrum Press with a very interesting list, almost entirely of Americans neglected in America—when you say that these were people with names like Louis Zukofsky, Robert Duncan, and Gary Snyder, you realise you're talking about a very strange period in American literature. These were books like New Directions books which were temporarily out of print, or things which British publishers had taken an option on and not taken up—it was the late sixties and people were going to read poetry. So he built up a list of people like that. He added the Englishman Basil Bunting who was terribly neglected and who'd just written *Briggflattts,* and was opening up again. And he added me. He published my little prose work *The Ship's Orchestra.* And then made a collection of the older pieces. So I published with him. And when I shook myself out of my block around 1970 I fairly rapidly wrote a prose work called 'The Cut Pages', from which this 'Stopped Frames and Set-Pieces' comes. And I put together another collection called *Matrix.* Those felt natural books to be doing.

JT: Were they with a mainstream press?

RF: I suppose the mainstream press, as England regards itself, has always been Faber. Fulcrum was not in a sense an experimental or avant garde press. It knew very well what it thought was quality. And it knew very well what it thought was going to be part of the literary history of the times. So it could reach out for Americans at full stretch, or in full flight, as [Robert] Duncan was at that time, and say 'This we can endorse. This we can use.' It would at the same time publish a certain number of chancey people like Spike Hawkins, Jeff Nuttall, the early Lee Harwood, and Christopher Middleton who was always getting knocked by English critics for being formalist and aesthetic—'Why can't you play one that we know? Why can't you play one we can all sing along with?'—the typical English critical cry. Fulcrum would do that. It was a serious press, which did quite nice books. And Americans bought them. As well as some English people. When I went to America I met all the people who had bought my Fulcrum books. They hired me to do readings. That's where my Fulcrum books were, on American bookshelves, in houses on campuses. People who'd bought them in the late sixties.

Eric Mottram: Does this mean that you are the kind of writer that sets himself procedures to work into, and that you hadn't found the procedures that were going to lead you to the next thing—would that be a way of saying it?

RF: Not entirely. I think the procedures are secondary to your state at the time; to the sort of man you are and the sort of life you are leading, and what you expect to happen next. Now, I never work very far ahead in any case, I never plan work very far ahead, and I like to work by the moment; and if I am writing, then I'm writing, and if I'm not, I'm very definitely not writing at all or having anything to do with it, and I think that I don't find it difficult to devise procedures which make it possible for me simply to be writing, but I don't find it easy to devise procedures which make me write happily; I'm not a great producer and I don't much enjoy the feeling of mere production.

EM: I was just thinking of this in the blurb of *Matrix*: 'Almost without exception my poems are propositions or explorations rather than reactions to personal experience.'

It seems to suggest that you work to certain poetic procedures. Then you say: 'The poems are to do with getting about in the mind and I tackle that in any way I can. I have to got from one cluster of ideas to another without a scaffolding of logic or narrative but I want to make the transitions within the terms of what I call poetry. I take it that the way a poem moves is the index of where the feeling in it lies.'

Now that is why I asked you about the procedures, because it looks as if you don't rely on personal experience to pressurise you into writing poetry.

RF: No. I stick to that throughout the whole of my writing. I think I've never written anything, certainly never written anything that I've kept, that was a straight reaction to an event, anything in the world; poems are meant to be just poems. That book I wrote after I was through the block and working again, and it characterised, I think, pretty well everything I'd done; but it doesn't mean that I have in fact a set of programmes for being writing. It means that when I do write, the writings are of writing rather than of the world, or any kind of reportage.

EM: Then you go on to say that one origin and basis of 'Matrix' was: 'one of those curious, near-hallucinatory experiences in which one is able to stand outside one's mind and watch its oddly assorted memories quickly reprogramming themselves to make new forms. On this occasion there was a rain of images which seemed to be joining one another, according to some logic of their own; they were nearly all to do with works of art.'

Then you say that you are concerned with 'forming relationships which I should never have presumed to try to improve on consciously', that the poems of the sequence are a sort of tour of its interior. That suggests, that in a sense you are relying on personal experience, perhaps quite heavily, but it is also very near surrealism, isn't it?

RF: It is very near surrealism, for which I have a great deal of sympathy. That was pretty exceptional, the poem 'Matrix' itself, in that it was almost the product of delayed thinking or waking dream which is an unusual sort of experience for me. It was quite literally as if certain alignments were made in the mind, chiefly by the fact that I had been writing a lot, and as it happened, the mental experience came within a few minutes; I was for once able to leave the inner experience for some months until I had some time to write it.

EM: Was there anything to do with automatic writing in connection with this? Do you understand the meaning of that?

RF: Yes, I understand a meaning for automatic writing, and I can't do it. I have done a few things in automatic writing which I think are not of much interest to anybody else, and they are not in the main line of what I do. The only things of that sort which are published, which are verbally automatic, are 'Three Early Pieces', which I at last let out last year, in a pamphlet. I forgot that. A little Transgravity pamphlet, which is the only thing of mine I know is in the shops: that is, around in some shops. That was verbal automatism; it was a long time ago; it is much the earliest.

EM: What's the date of that, then?

RF: The work was written in, I think, 1954. There is nothing else in print that is earlier than about 1957. But there is a distinction here which I was just starting to make, which I've lost again.

EM: It's about the automatic writing and the surrealist techniques.

RF: Yes. The surrealist thing: certainly I got some of my earliest kicks from surrealist work and I'm very sympathetic to it.

EM: For instance, what?

RF: For instance pictures—Ernst particularly, Yves Tanguy, anything I ever read of Tzara, anything of Picabia.

EM: You used to have, as far as I can remember, beside your mantelpiece in Birmingham, a little Duchamp work—what was it ...

RF: It was just a picture of Duchamp.

EM: That's right, does that mean anything in particular for you?

RF: Duchamp is a major ethical figure for me, and a major marker of the sort of inherent qualities of the aesthetic you make when you work. The narrow line he trod with the ready-mades and the way his own life moved around the trail of his works, both made and found, and presented very narrowly, clearly marked for me one of the boundary lines of what you do when you make art. But I didn't know anything about Duchamp until, I suppose, I was over thirty, you know, when neo-Dada became popular with the public in England. I didn't know about him until then.

EM: Did you know about John Cage?

RF: I first heard about Cage in 1959. I first knew work by Cage later than that.

EM: I was thinking of the metamorphosis and 'changes' ideas connected with your work. Was the idea of jazz changes involved at any point in your work? I am interested in the relationship between the music and the poetry, if there is any, consciously, in your life.

RF: There is very little direct relation indeed, although I would say that, if I were put to it, jazz music has been more important to me for longer than poetry has. I was trying to play jazz many years before I started writing poetry, and although I had never done so much publicly, in terms of the fact that it hadn't got so far, let's face it, as the poetry, I spent far more time with jazz music than I have with poetry.

EM: Forgive me if I say this, it might sound very rude, but I don't intend to be – I've not heard you play professional jazz, I've only heard you play privately on your piano and mine, and it doesn't seem to me that you have a distinctive jazz piano style, like you have a distinctive poetic style, that you seem to be more imitative.

RF: That's right. This is a matter of the stage that one's taken to. As a piano player I've always been ... I'm a jazz fan who plays the piano. I could always earn money and work very nicely as a band member and an accompanist. I was perfectly capable of that, but I never, apart from very early days, when I played a lot as a schoolboy, I never was committed to thinking that I could define style and control the circumstance. There is one rather important thing here, which is probably not a matter of talent but a matter of circumstances: that in poetry your work may get nowhere at all; it may stay in a drawer for ten years, no-one may know anything about it; but quite simply if you are acting or if you are playing music, you have got to get a hall, acoustics, hearers, side-men and instruments in tune and so forth; and quite straightforwardly, the conditions were appalling that I was trying to play music in.

EM: But you did play with some really good jazz people from the States, didn't you, who came to Birmingham, so your experience is professional.

RF: Yes, we all did that.

EM: Who did you play with, do you remember any?

RF: They were chiefly British people, and Bud Freeman, among others. I used to work for them in the kind of late-traditional jazz club and little modern groups. We were constantly working with people like Tony Coe, Don Rendell, Danny Moss, you know the ordinary London soloists; but in every provincial city the local people do that.

EM: But this has a very big effect, doesn't it, on *The Ship's Orchestra* ? The feel of being part of a jazz group from day to day is very strong there. Did you not play that part of your experience into *The Ship's Orchestra* ?

RF: Not much. There were one or two things, there were one or two scenes, such as the Dancing Slipper Ballroom in West Bridgford, do you know that place? It is a marvellous—well, you don't have to know it, it's just a beautiful location which from the Sixties would be merely chic, but that was earlier than the Sixties: just a place by Trent Bridge Cricket Ground that we would go to and work, and the kids waited in a queue in the street—a Lyon's shop built in the 1970's with a dancing studio over the top run by, I take it, a pair of championship formation dancers and a little ballroom with a bar; and literally there was the bandstand in *The Ship's Orchestra*, a semicircular object. It actually had black lino on it and a rim around it and high heeled shoe marks all round it. That sort of thing was at the Dancing Slipper Ballroom in West Bridgford, just the tat, but in fact the whole point of *Ship's Orchestra* was that I had never been a professional musician and I'd never been on a ship.

EM: I meant that feel of the group, and the way they talk, to each other, seems to me an inside thing; it feels like it, that it's something you know about.

RF: That just gets fed in by the way; the actual starter for that, which probably doesn't show in the book at all, is Picasso's picture, *Three Musicians*, you know the one where there are three clown-like figures, one of whom has a black clarinet; and who is to say that there are not four musicians? The whole question about what they are, are they there, how many are there, what plans are they in, are they features of sound or of dimension, and so forth; I just started with that as the conundrum and then fed my own aesthetic through into it, which is made up of this dance hall tat—which I love, of course. I was really happy in a sense to be a schoolmaster and college lecturer in a suit by day, and by night to be cut off from the door of the room I was working in by a lot of sort of knife-brandishing customers and to be playing for strippers and tattooed women, and things of this sort. It was all right, it was a change.

EM: That ship is interesting to me for another reason: again and again in your work there is a dramatisation of a need to be in some kind of small isolated area, an island or a ship or room – is that not true? Are you conscious of that?

RF: Oh, yes, very conscious.

EM: Particularly in 'Matrix' itself.

RF: The island?

EM: Yes, and the garden.

RF: Yes.

EM: This occurs again and again—and the names of those plants.

RF: Well, yes, those are accurate.

EM: You are a gardener among other things; you like gardening, do you not?

RF: Yes, I do like that sort of thing. I wouldn't be heavy about it, and I know you're not being heavy about it, but I wouldn't be heavy about the mythology; I just take it for granted that one mythologises, that whatever one talks about has got body analogues all the time, that what I talk about has got body analogues all over it, because I'm a committed puritanical sensualist; I want to talk about body imagery.

EM: 'Metamorphosis' is like that is it not?

RF: Yes. I'm actually dissolving bodies and creating bodies in that, in and out of things which are not bodies.

EM: One of the things you are awfully good at when you are playing the piano and in conversation, is mimicry. You have the knack of imitating anybody you have heard; and I've once heard you read a faked Swedish, Bergman soundtrack poem. Have you ever tried mimicry seriously in poetry, using parodies or pastiche, in your published work?

RF: Yes, but not in a published work.

EM: What do you do it for, exercises or fun or ... ?

RF: Sheer bloody malice.

EM: That sounds more like it.

RF: Why not? I've never gone into it, I suppose the motives here are rather base; I love style, I am fascinated by what it is, apart from the basic ego drive that makes artists work, and the high ethics that they have and the calling and all this. I'm fascinated by the way in which that drive gets differentiated and gets personalised in the features of the personality that are used, and people begin to imitate themselves. This always fascinates me in all the arts, and I like

53

to reduce things to caricature and it is sometimes something I have to watch against, if I want to leave people that I read or like free to exist. The Bergman thing was in fact a sort of mock Swedish thing, it was a sort of product; I've never published it simply because nobody's ever wished to print it. People just rejected it. It is an imitation of what happens to you when you watch a lot of Ingmar Bergman films and read the subtitles and just hear that Swedish thing when you know not a word of Swedish. It was a conversation between two people about crucifying nymphs, crucifying girls in the woods and things of this kind. I once read it at the I.C.A. and I said merrily 'Is there a Swede in the house?' and a bloke put his hand up and said: 'I'm Swedish'; I read it all the same. He came up afterwards, all menacingly, and said 'It was a very good impression of Swedish, but I cannot make out what you really think of Ingmar Bergman'; I said 'I think Bergman is very strong, a very strong director, but I have certain reservations'. He looked at me very hard, with very cold blue eyes, and said 'In Sweden we admire Ingmar Bergman very much'. And that was that.

EM: One thing further before we go on to one or two publishing matters. How do you feel about a puzzle factor in poetry; I mean that the invitation to read a poem may be similar to an invitation to enter into a puzzle, into a problem scene. That is, you give so much information to the reader to enter, invitatorily, into that scene, then leave it, and then densify the sort of labyrinth or puzzle area.

RF: You mean I do this?

EM: Do you do this? There is a puzzle factor a great deal in your work. With *The Ship's Orchestra*, for instance, one has to make certain, one has to discover, what the connections between the sections are.

RF: Yes.

EM: And in *City* too, I think.

RF: Yes. If I can just put a disclaimer here, that *City* is an assemblage which was not in all its versions assembled by me; but in the later works, in *The Ship's Orchestra* and the poem 'Matrix', I don't very often knowingly allow myself references which aren't within the poem. In 'Matrix' I certainly did—I know there are things to do with Thomas Mann's *Dr Faustus*, Monet's waterlily paintings; these seem to me to be easily available works of art; they are in Penguin, as it were.

EM: And the Böcklin picture?

54

RF: And the Böcklin picture, which I would have thought most people know—I don't know.

EM: I wondered about that.

RF: But I have also allowed myself to deal with things that no-one can know because they are rolled up in a cupboard, in my house. Basically I would aim to make a surface, which may be rather heavily impacted, but which is centrally the given, the thing, that anybody who picks it up to read has to play with. I would go so far as to say that I would be inimical to ever writing—and I don't very much like reading—things which posit a sort of area of shared civilisation, any of the versions of Bloomsbury, whether it is in New York, or Paris or wherever it may be popping up, which do posit the idea that civilisation ever existed. In my book, it hasn't.

EM: It seems to me that the procedures that one is invited to follow in your poetry separate you quite considerably from a great deal of poetry since 1946, and I was wondering if you had anything to say about the reasons why it took some time for you to be well-known in this country. For instance, I am thinking particularly of *City*, or part of *City*, coming out in *Kulchur*. In that same issue, and I think the issue that followed, Denise Levertov wrote something about the condition of British poetry in which you and Michael Shayer and Gael Turnbull, and one or two others, were like star-performers, against everybody that the *TLS* and *The Observer* and so on, were keen on. Then Gael Turnbull placed you in a context (in an article that followed) with Basil Bunting, who at that time had been completely forgotten except by the one or two people who recognised his excellence. You seem to have belonged, as far as they are both concerned, to a group of poets who were hardly known in many ways in this country.

RF: You didn't have to belong to a group to be hardly known.

EM: What do you think about that?

RF: I can only speak ... is it of interest to speak historically about this?

EM: I think it is very important, Roy.

RF: Obviously, some people in this room were around. It's that, as I saw it, you were either on the main line, and to be a bit blunt about it, you went straight from Oxford or Cambridge into London and you headed for Faber and Faber or you got into John Lehmann's pocket; but there was the usual narrowness of access to work. In those days there was no underground that I knew of, there was no cyclostyled, no mimeographed stuff, and in so far as one got any model of what literary activity was, it was that somehow or other one sent off poems to the editor of *The Listener* and so on, you know—you did what it said in the *Writers' and Artists' Year Book*. You sent off this sort of stuff, and, of course, you got it back or you never heard of it again. Poems were used as column breakers or you got as I got after a certain long time, an actual note from John Lehmann on the rejections slip saying 'Frightfully interesting; so sorry I haven't got room'. Well, I did that, and we must all have done that, and good gracious me, I can remember writing poems that would cut no ice, in fact; they were not accomplished, they were tentative, they were semi-surrealist, semi-romantic, all sorts of things, and later they were, when I started to find ways of working that interested me, more Black Mountain, more surrealist and so forth, and much less like the people of my generation who made it, that is Thom Gunn and Ted Hughes—that's my age group. But these were not poems that were visible to the people who had the editorial chairs.

EM: Why not?

RF: Why not? Well, that's their privilege.

Jed Rasula: You often deal with things in your work in terms of archetypes: *City* and *The Ship's Orchestra* are full of details, but not with the kind of information that would normally tie a work down to a particular locality in time. Do you think this is a matter of conscious attention to the particulars of your subject matter, or whether there is something else involved? In other words, that the essential material is gotten at most readily by a suspension of temporal ties and attention to details of locality?

RF: I'm interested in getting an effect of indeterminacy in those things. Most of the *City* writing is meant to be about a city which has already turned into a city of the mind. Where the writing is topographical it's meant to do with the EFFECTS of topography, the creation of scenic moments, psychological environments, and it's not meant to be an historical/spatial city entailed to empirical reality. With *The Ship's Orchestra* there is a very particular exercise of that sort going on. Because it was a thing devised to be a study of people on a ship. Which is a thing I'd never done, I hadn't travelled on a ship. I had no intention of ever doing so, particularly, and I have no knowledge of maritime matters at all. And I chose the ship very particularly, not as a symbol or archetype of a voyage, although the book is full (I hope) of jokes about the archetype of voyage, and so on and so on. But in that book, yes, I wanted to be writing about something I didn't know about, which was not entailed to any sort of reality and which was in fact made up of all kinds of fantastic impressions: you know, it was a ship off a movie, a ship out of children's illustrations, a ship out of other people's poems, that sort of thing. And that is for me very important—to make it fairly clear without making lurid effects, and make it fairly clear that the thing that's being written is an artifact, is to do with the subjective.

JR: *The Ship's Orchestra* has struck me as interesting in its similarities with John Ashbery's *Three Poems*. Both books—and this is more where the similarity lies—have an extreme sort of concentration which is like wringing water out of a washcloth, wringing something dry. And the striking contrast though is that your work is developed around things and Ashbery's around ideas. The 'thinking' in *The Ship's Orchestra* seems to me to proceed on the level of perceptual attentions rather than any sort of logic or cohesion of thought as a logical process. And I wonder if it would be off the mark to say that by directing your efforts to the things on the ship and by lifting any specific temporal identities the work comes over to a reader as functioning on a level of archetypes?

RF: Archetypes? Because I deal with things which could hold archetypal significance, you mean? Instead of turning it into a discourse about the things?

JR: Right.

RF: If I could perhaps answer that in two parts. Yes, I certainly accept that I work by perceptual attentions. For me the thing had to be grounded in sensations and in refinements of sensation, and indeed the book is written as an elaboration of almost hallucinatory sensory effects—tactile, olfactory, visual of course, auditory. And the book in fact has a fairly simple base vocabulary of colours, substances, things like grey mucus, saline tastes, things which are body tastes, body sensations, and things in the world. And it's an exploration of familiar body sensations extended throughout a small perceived world. And any intellectual play that takes place is meant to be seen as a possibly futile, bemusing, almost certainly erroneous play over the commands of a rule of sensation. That's partly because I don't have any training in logic or any education in abstract thinking or any inclination towards it. I've got a great distrust of it. And, you know, partly through sheer pleasure in wanting to write a book which expounded a very limited register of sensations and make it more and more elaborate until it could rapidly generate characters and generate action and make sort of turns on its own.
        So that's why it's different from the Ashbery thing. As for how it moves towards an archetypal reading, I don't know. If I was to catch hold of seeing anything like that as I wrote I would almost certainly want to make a joke of it, or simply (and I think I did this, in fact) include or envelop the archetypal reading into the ordinary play of ideas. And in fact I think on the first page there's a little brief vision of Billy Budd's feet dangling out of heaven, which in one sense is meant to signal that I know all about Melville, you know, the moment we set to sea. And I know all about.... That sounds arrogant, but I mean I'm aware of the great ladder of authority the moment I start talking

about any sort of hierarchy or any sort of achievement or any kind of judgement or justice.

I think really the point about this is that in the writing I'm not interested in making a structure which has got a climax, a thing which has got an authoritarian centre, a rule or mandate somewhere in its middle which the work will unfold and will reach. I'm much more interested in simply.... Not writing towards a middle but making all the possible ways of accounting for this perceptual attention, this perceptual field, I'm making all the possible ways of accounting for its fight for survival, take their own chance one with another, without any sort of hierarchal thing. So while I wouldn't deny that maybe if any feeling comes up in a piece of writing like that it might be because I'm quite happy to appeal, if you like, to archetypal things because we must, because they're there, they're in the vocabulary of all the things we do. They're not structural, they're incidental. There are passages that tend toward the general, the exemplary. There's a bit where somebody's had a baby, given birth to a child inside an airplane tyre. And all right, the airplane tyre is a female orifice maybe, maybe not—it could be a house or a dwelling, it could be a pathetic statement. But there is a baby and it's quite intentional really that there should be a feeling of pathos, of emotion, towards birth and the naked babe at that point. It's not a key, though, it's an incidental thing which is fed in and generated by my feeling at the time.

The other thing to say about the piece of writing is that, along with a lot of things I do, it was rigorously composed in an additive form. That is, each section was written in an attempt to refer only to what I had already written in that work, and without any drive forward at all. It's not a work of pure method, but to get a starter and then to recycle, reprogramme the thinking, the mental sensations of what had gone before, and see what the field that I had laid down was in fact spawning and producing, and then to stop and to see what, let's say the first four parts plus the fifth part which I'd just written—what that bred. And then I'd write the sixth and then I'd see what parts 1 to 6 bred. So if anything came up with any structural look to it, it could only have a structural leverage as long as that.

Mike Erwin: In a poem 'For Realism' in *Collected Poems 1968* you write, 'A conscience / builds, late, on a ridge. A realism / tries to record, before they're gone, / what silver filth these drains have run'. Does that indicate a sort of a feeling on your part of responsibility for public welfare or sociological concern, in a sense? That you try to engender in your poetry?

RF: I don't do that very often. That poem in fact has more social comment to do with a particular moment than I usually employ. But one thing that I would like to be able to do, as a sort of technical problem, is to make a double use of the ordinary data of sense. That is, to write about, shall we say, a city which exists in space and time and has a name and is not a city which is already mentalised or internalised in the way I was describing in my answer to your first question. I would like to be able to use names, to name names, not as brute documentation, not as a brute documentary thing, but to have floated real things into a fictive world and use them without distancing them at all. Anyway, in that particular poem I had it in mind that very often in trying to evoke urban things I had as it were dissolved things and made them strange so that I was free from the entailments of them in ordinary reality, so that I could in fact use them within the compass of my own perceptual thinking, my own way of working. The conscience I had was that this was always distorting, which I accepted. But I had an ambition to make the transaction so clean that I could just take from a thing—a street with a name to it—sufficient properties to exist verbally in my poem and at the same time to be answerable to the reality should anybody so and look at it. I was writing about a street people could recognise, but I still was writing about a street that was in my poem and not just stupidly reported as it might be. In a very ordinary piece of documentary. Now, that explains why in that poem, unusually for me, I take an actual scene (streets with names to them, things which more or less happened as they're reported, a particular hour, particular time and consequently a particular moment in urban rebuilding)—they are pulling the place down and they are building the flats. And this was a place which was real to me, a place with family association. I think the business about social responsibility comes in very simply, in that you only had to be in that place and look at that thing and you'd really got a symbolised landscape ready-made for you; you'd got a Victorian slum full of a particular sort of life which could be turned into metaphor, i.e. the silver filth thing, which is a visual and moral metaphor. And over this scraped hill these flats were being built and put in the poem; but I took it as read that the blocks of the flats were built on intellectual models of the people who were going to be moved into them, they were built graphed, all the ordinary little hopes and quite large corruptions of urban polities and contract tampering and this sort of business. Without going into details, without knowing any details, you just got a nationwide/worldwide picture of the way these things are done. It was just a counter. For me that's an assumptions it's not a social poem as such. It's not meaning to make a social point but to assume the social point. Somebody who would read my poem, I would imagine, would see the scene much that way. And the use of the word 'conscience' there is simply sceptical, that conscience is what makes the people who run a big city, the people who are in public life, whatever makes people go into public life, what they do. If you like, it's conscience, it's blood money, it's reformism. But it's a term like any other.

ME: You don't feel a strong urgency though, in general, to encounter temporal problems and work into them through your poetry, other than a sort of anonymous centre of humanity in the city, and so forth?

RF: You mean to write activist or political poetry?

ME: In a sense, yes.

RF: No, I don't. This is largely a matter of language, and the relation of language to perception. There are a lot of people who have the social view on general issues that I might have. It's very commonly accessible. Social views or political views tend to get interesting when they're apocalyptic, and mine aren't apocalyptic. So they don't naturally take the form of images. But as a poet I'm an image maker, and I wouldn't sloganise a mass of really quite scattered or branching or complicated reactions to social matters; I wouldn't want to sloganise them into an image. I don't think it's any use for the sort of writer I am to do that. If your image is capable of being moralised, in this country particularly, it will be. The moral will be screwed out of it. I deplore this; it's a simplifying tendency. In this country people take a little bit of poetry, a little bit of literature, and if there's a moral in it, however crude, it will be taken, it will be coarsened still further, it'll be used and remembered and used and remembered over and over again. And people stop reading, people stop attending. And I'm very wary about writing even single poems which could be the rallying point of my own little area of work. A sort of hit single among the things I've written. For my taste I moralise too much already.

ME: Do you find then that the things you're working with and the kind of filth and corruption that you encounter in, for example, the poem 'For Realism' that you mention, is that kind of thing, do you think, in a timeless centre throughout the history of man? Are the problems and situations that we're in that you're working on not temporally bound, but continuous without modulation?

RF: I don't think of them like that. They're certainly historical matters, and they can be ideologically plotted. And I suppose in thinking about them ecologically, socially, I would use that kind of technique, thinking about them. You know, hypocrisy, idealism and so forth, they're going to come out of certain predisposing things which are large movements, which are historically/ culturally visible. I don't see them in terms of any abiding ethic.

I think, insofar as any of this comes out in the poems, it would be that the poems obviously are sceptical in all sorts of ways. They're sceptical formulations of life, systemisations; the poems are anarchic. The poems represent, if you like, an anarchic response to—not so much social issues, things which come out of society and which stand out and can be put in newspapers—but to the whole rubble, the whole mass of tiny interfaced circumstances that carry you along, make the present in which you exist. In that field, I haven't any sense of an ahistorical ethic. I mean, my heroes are people like Schweik and Brecht, heroes who are committed to strange pragmatic reactions to circumstances even against their own interests.

JR: Your work has been largely oriented around consciousness of place: the city, the ship, interiors (with various figures), 'Matrix', the 'Glenthorne' sequence. Have you been influenced by American efforts in this direction: Olson, Ginsberg, Dorn? In 'The Six Deliberate Acts', in *Matrix*, are the lines 'The more he looked / the more he saw.' I'd like to ask about the notion of place as central perceptive location. By that I mean, that a necessary function of a man's developing sensibility to himself is his sensitivity to environment. Does this have something to do with your use of place in your works, your manner of making the act of writing an act of seeing more?

RF: Several parts to that. I've been told that I've been influenced by Americans. An enormous number of people come to mind, some American, some not. You might just as well, for me, talk about Rilke's Paris or Kafka's Prague or the imaginary towns that Paul Klee made up or Kokoschka's paintings of towns he worked in. That is, my sense of place is a very—I won't say it's an ordinary, but maybe it's a childlike sense of place. A matter of simple appetite. An idea that places may be rich in various ways. Bits of places may subdivide into further bits of places. It's a very simple relation to appetite.

Fascination with a location—I don't want to duck out too hard from the American tag here, but it could as well be those little bits you get at the back of Italian primitive paintings, the cities on hilltops, as any sort of possibly theoretical concern with place, such as you get in Olson or Ed Dorn. That sort of work seems to me to be very necessary for them. And those two, very particularly, USE the idea of location in America inevitably quite differently from the way in which any Englishman COULD use a sense of location, or could use a sort of game of time axis versus place axis. It's meaningful for me as I read them. But not for me. I mean, it's commonplace to say that for an Englishman looking at place, compared to an American his thing has got to be historical. He's only got to look out of his window and something a few hundred years old is going to stick through his awareness. And you can see this, even in my own small migration from a city to this rural, fairly rural, sort of place. I've become much more aware of history, and I take a good deal of pleasure in seeing the medieval or the very English things of hundreds and hundreds of years of, say, farming. I'm interested in this. But that's a matter of very ordinary interest.

When I was writing the *City* poems, and particularly this is when I was first writing with any sort of sense of something that I must do for myself (and this was around the time of late 20's, time of being 30); when I was doing that I quite simply had a sense of place which was not culturally extensive, it didn't extend into history at all, even though in the *City* pieces I invoke the 19th century culture versus the 20th century culture. But historically that's very simple, it's really of very little subtlety, and it doesn't, as it were, attempt to invoke the historical meaning of the behaviour of the people on the ground in anything like the way Olson does.

What I was faced with was something quite personal, which was the sensation of having lived for a very long time (and I'm not a traveller at all, I stay very much in one place), having lived for a very long time in and having had my consciousness of, a particular large nondescript undesigned environment which was, as it happened, an expanding industrial city, which was a deposit of all sorts of inadvertent by-products of ideas. In many cases the cultural ideas, the economic ideas, had disappeared into the graveyards of people who had the ideas. But the by-products in things like street layouts, domestic architecture, where the schools were, how anything happened—all these things were left all over the place as a sort of script, an indecipherable script with no key. And the interesting thing for me was that the culture, particularly the metropolitan culture, the literary culture, had no alphabet to offer for simply talking about what I saw all the time. I mean, when I say in *City*, 'most of it's never been seen', it's a provocative phrase: it wasn't verbalised, it wasn't talked about. And there I wasn't interested really at all in the particular city, but in the phenomenon of having a perceptual environment which was taken as read, which was taken to be assumed and not a thing for which any vocabulary needed to exist. Consequently in historical terms that needed only to be very thin. I was talking about really my own time. And in the work I'd be bouncing the feelings I had, which were the feelings of a rather belated adolescence. I was coming back to the city in my late twenties at a time when it was being rebuilt. And I was also in a state of life when I could remember childhood—I was far enough away from childhood to have an intensity about some memories. And again I'd had a fairly inarticulate childhood, a childhood where I had a lot of sensations going in, but not a very—you know, I wasn't a child writer or anything of that sort, a child reader. There were still things left in my own perception which were unsorted. And there was another thing which was again merely personal—my father was dying, and he was very closely associated with the city, with these areas over a period of forty years. Seeing this life ending, and the inevitable process of turning up old photographs, old apprenticeship papers, extended time that made you realise more than usually how much the place was dependent upon very evanescent, temporal, subjective renderings of it, which might never BE rendered. And at that point my own lifetime was extended through his.

Really the place in there is a way of exploring inner space rather than in any way attempting to do justice either to the place as itself or to having any large conception of place. I can only say that as a non-traveller I take it for granted that if I were to have set up in late youth or early manhood or even now to trot the globe and be an exile and never stay in one place I couldn't get out of my blood the fact which I fairly recently worked out, which is that until I was 13 years old I didn't sleep a night outside the city of Birmingham, for one reason or another. And probably only spent a couple of nights outside the house I was born in. And I lived in the house I was born in until I was 23. This mere factor of having gone outside the city into the countryside or to nearby towns only for the day, coming back at night, this was the sort of people we were. And even then going fairly short distances for very short periods—that quite heavy inertia and if you like accidental, though it doesn't sound accidental, it sounds like a sort of psychosis—there's a circumstantial adherence to one place with the consequent inevitability of having your mind made up enormously of impressions like that. It's where I was at, what I had to work with.

JR: In 'The Glenthorne Poems' talking about trees, you say, 'This is how it was when first I started with poetry // They are already three-parts idea'. I wonder whether this is related to Williams' notion of 'no ideas but in things', or even if it isn't, what your further sense of that is?

RF: The trouble with no ideas but in things is that it has become an idea. And it's an idea I do quite cheerfully talk about in seminars on Carlos Williams, and that is perhaps a betrayal of old Bill. Not the idea, but the wealth and diversity of sensations taken from, again, a limited immediate perceptual field, is something which appeals to me enormously in Williams just as a writer. The doctrine of ideas in things is the nearest to a slogan of any poetic slogan that I'd want to carry around, that I WOULD want to carry around, but I wouldn't want to carry it around all that much, because it can just turn into a thing to hit myself over the head with. And no, if I were in a certain way at a particular time I would feel it doctrinally quite sensible to have an exciting vocabulary, a vocabulary which was exciting to me and which was very abstract. I could quite happily set myself the task of starting with an idea and generating sensations. There's one poem—in fact, there are two poems which do this to some extent. They are 'Ceremonial Poems' in the *Collected Poems*, and there's particularly one that starts off, 'Absolute pity advancing. . . .' and this really says that I find it diverting to think, if you like in a French way, of a sort of exemplary figure. I can't think about pity, as if it belonged to theology, which is for me a hoax area. I can only think of it as art, and if you look at that poem, I immediately turn pity into an artistic composition—artistic in inverted commas—it's a sort of crummy classical art which then gradually breaks and flows in all sorts of ways towards MY sensibility which is where my things are. So an idea has to come into my sensibility before I can entertain it. But to be doctrinal about it I suppose I would say that I am chiefly interested in hauling words towards concreteness. Not a stylistic concreteness—I'm not so much bothered at this stage with the Pound precepts about clarity of image and so forth, although those have gone in fairly deep for me. But with referring EVERYTHING to bodily existence, as simply as that, you know, referring language to it, the counters of language as a sort of sensory register.
    'The Trees', if I can say something about that. Here I have to get off the little podium I just built, in that while wanting to recreate, to assert the physicality of life, I also have to cope with a visual memory which is hallucinatory to a stupefying degree. And the fact that a lot of one's sensations are very heavy and very hard to shift and very hard to manipulate and I'm perfectly capable of getting myself in certain situations into a perceptual field which is just

jammed solid with sensory data, and there is no discourse at all, no movement in it. I can sometimes have visual memory which looks like a colour slide. And the difficulty is sometimes simply to stalk up on it, to break it up, to find some way of realising the subjectivity, the relative instability of the impressions, to stop them solidifying, turning into a collection of colour slides or a gallery of sensations. And making them mobile. And I find this very hard to express. But there are some artists, some sorts of artists, who seem to me to have remarkable freedom for simply SEEING things m they are in the world and rendering them naturally, without either becoming formalist or becoming stupefyingly realistic. These are all sorts of people—it's a matter of pace and scale. I think people like Gogol, people like Hiroshige, people who would sketch and have a thing which looked as though it had existed in the real world and had its own independence and its own life and its own value. But also one dimension of its existence was that it was to be made into a picture, it lived as a picture. And 'The Trees', without being a cliché, a pictorial cliché or a poetic cliché, those trees for me had the look (or at least I had the feeling) of being able to see them as if they were already digested and packed for language. Of course what it comes down to is that the whole thing is a matter of set, or whether your own eye, your own look at things is light and mobile enough to be able to take them and handle them. Williams, of course, all his life pretty much, had the most superb technique of not settling, of not embedding himself in system. Or at least in a large amount of the work he seems to me to have strategies—he's very well aware that he needs strategy for keeping moving in ideas and sensations.

ME: I'm wondering what you think about the case of poetry more often sheltering and protecting people than stimulating them and opening them up? If that is the case.

RF: As far as I see it, a poem has business to exist, really, if there's a reasonable chance that somebody may have his perceptions rearranged by having read it or having used it. The poem is always capable of being a subversive agent, psychologically, sensuously, however you like. If you make that requirement of every poem you get very few poems. This may be one reason why I don't write many. I think I would say unless a poem is making some kind of potentially new dislocative effect in the minds of some readers—you don't know which of your particular poems are even going to be picked up by anybody, used for what purpose by whom, you can't tell this, and my way of figuring it is that you make certain bids, you release certain items, you leave them around and wonder what will happen to them.

Certainly a poem can, if you like, comfort, it can glorify the culture to which it belongs. I'm not at all interested in this. I'm not at all interested in very discursive poetry, I'm very suspicious of poetry which can be embraced by people who are interested in, as it were, identifying a culture as a culture at a particular moment. It may just as well get on with making things new. The thing you say about what poetry can do—sheltering—you mean sheltering people from perception, sheltering people from what is new?

ME: Arranging perception in such a way that it's pleasing, or at least....

RF: It can do that in all sorts of ways; it can make pictures, it can make a surrogate personality in the poet's self, you know, make a structure of intrusive personality which shelters people or gives them a vicarious self to live through, like any movie star or famous suicide or whatever. That, I think, is illusory as well, and it's romantic, tiredly so.

JR: Is there anything that you conceive of or are conscious of in your own work as making an attempt to keep people who read your work from any sort of falsifying interpretation or reaction to it which is more of a sheltering than a stimulating?

RF: No. Simple answer—it's more complicated than that. In things which (it sounds strange to say) things I've had a fair degree of control over—that is, longer works, *Ship's Orchestra* and *Cut Pages* which of course are works written on a principle of unpredictability, paradoxically enough were the works where I felt I had a clear control over the composition. And the stuff in the two later books and *The Ship's Orchestra* very much. But those are things which are read, insofar as they're read at all, on the whole by people who know what they're reading. There are things in the *Collected Poems* which are read by people I would think of as less skilled readers. There are things which get in anthologies. I have a curious stake in the writing business here. And it's a very simple problem. If I write work that can't be taken as merely comforting, but is if you like sincere, if I only publish that, my viability will be even less than it is. Not many people have read *The Ship's Orchestra*; fewer people have read *The Cut Pages*. I think it's a pity, I think people might enjoy *The Ship's Orchestra* if they read it. But when I wrote it I thought it might be ten people. There have been more than that. But what happens to me is that I do get people, more people as it were, reading me with more energy because I have written about an industrial city, because I've written at least one simple narrative poem about some of my relatives getting killed in an air-raid. It's the thing most untypical of anything I believe about poetry that I ever wrote. But it's the poem which has been most reprinted, and which people remember and like to hear at a reading. And if I give a reading I like to see there's somebody out there, and I'm not an oral poet; but I like to show up, stand up and be counted with my own book in my hand. In the way of readings, a poem with a narrative and a moral, or at least a narrative and a joke, whatever you like, is going to make contact in a way in which passages from *The Cut Pages* are not. But I could retreat entirely from the narrative and topographical without any regret. I don't compose in this mode now. But I tend to be somewhat saddled with representational things. And in a sense I don't too much regret having some works like that in the book, although I'm usually very aware of having them misused. I'm not meaning to sound patronising about people who like simpler poetry. I'm talking not about very inexperienced people who might just happen to walk into the reading and not be readers of poetry. I'm talking about critics, quite skilled readers who will very characteristically go at my work from the representational end or the end which appears to have morality in it, and might be what you could call comforting in that the poetry might be left and the concepts which it gives rise to can then be discussed away from the poetry.

But I suppose in things like *The Ship's Orchestra* or *The Cut Pages* there is a fairly simple, I would have thought, set of dramatic guides to say don't take this narrative too seriously, don't expect to be allowed to settle, if there's going to be a sex bit don't expect to know who it was doing it, or you can play with this if you like but I'm not going to give you biography or I'm not going to give you pornography or any kind of rallying cry: it's not going to come together. I would hope there are stylistic signals to that effect. Just as, you know, the central character of a Svevo novel is built to have a bit of indeterminacy about him. That's perhaps not the best example, but that sort of thing. The difficulty is, of course, to have this sort of indeterminate sense of consciousness without losing any hope of a reader at all except a reader who's addicted to your method.

ME: Does the presence of a reader intrude upon you much when you write a work?

RF: Put it this way, the only intrusion of a reader on my writing or putative reader is to stop me writing, blocks me completely. I can only write happily if I forget that anyone might read it or if I assume no one will or that it doesn't matter whether anyone will. Certainly, that's the way I have to operate. I think when I first realised about 1965 that anyone was reading me at all it stopped me writing for four or five years. And it was only when the books were published, late 60's, and got a little bit of currency that I found it possible to do a double-take and realise that I could write with somebody out there. But there's a personal thing to do with the kind of man I am. I got over stage-fright, and I now will quite happily read and don't mind publishing. But until I was nearly forty years old it was a source of mingled compulsion and excruciating pain to publish, in that I could never feel I had got the thing right, that I had the power of design, which I might be expected to have, and so on and so on and so forth. And it was only after doing a fairly small amount of work rather late in life that I got confidence to begin. And now I quite cheerfully go around and support my own productions. And people who don't like it, it's their loss. I don't worry about reactions.

ME: So you would continue to write for yourself if there was no possibility of an audience?

RF: I would, certainly. And if I become unpublishable I'd cheerfully go grass-roots and do what I'm always telling other people to do who write and say how can I get my books published by your publisher? Things like that. I tell them to go get working with the mimeo machine and give them away, and then do another and give that away. I do that. It doesn't matter to me. I don't make any money, well, not much. And I don't expect ever to. And, you know, it's 'Al Que Quiere', him as wants it can have it. I don't believe the world of the published book, or the world of the literary arena is very real. What is publication? It's a complicated series of things that happen or don't happen, but it's not a once-for-all thing. And if what looks like a system of having books printed breaks down, it's of no concern at all for me that it should do. And I don't know, for instance, if I should write another book like the four books I've done. I might forever on do pamphlets. And what I tend to do now, or what I've written since the books have come out, have been texts for art works which have come out in limited editions. Because I've enjoyed working with the artists. Or people write and say would I write a pamphlet, and they have a format which is so many pages and so many copies. And I'm perfectly likely to think it would have been nice to have filled one of those pamphlets. I would write a work that shape. On the other hand I might write a work that was shapeless. A thing I might do, I have it roughly in me to do a rewrite of—I've got a quarter of a century's worth of very formless notebooks, and I may simply do a rework, it may take me 25 years, of the notebooks to see what's in them and see what the rewriting of them means, if I live 25 years. But it wouldn't matter to me very much whether it turned into publishable units. At the moment people write me and ask me to give them bits of one sort of thing or another sort of thing which I usually don't have at hand at all. Having got to a stage of being publishable, I don't know what effect it would have on me if no one asked me to publish anything. But I probably would just make things and press them on people occasionally.

JR: Going back to some things you were saying about *The Ship's Orchestra* earlier, and the field of sensual impression there. A work like *The Ship's Orchestra* is in many ways an exploration of the limits and territories of the self and individual perceptions. There are such perceptions in there as the question 'What shape is the field of vision the eyes experience?' where, I think, in just a few words a good deal of the scaffolding of our way of looking at things is torn away. There necessarily has to be response to it on a reader's part if he's reading at all what's going on in the work itself. And I wonder if there's any connection between these kind of perceptions and your feelings about the subjective obstacle to objectivity?

RF: I don't know if they're systematically linked in my mind. They're ideas of a sort, the sort of ideas I have. No great strategy involved there, but this sort of problem or this sort of game is what occupies me. I don't find it a problem in the sense that one can't see, can't live, without solving it. I don't necessarily want to solve the problem, I merely want to play with the problem. There's a thing in Nabokov somewhere where he says that recollection is a prime artistic act, the prime activity of art; the human brain is only moderately well designed for exercising this. And for recollection you could substitute anything else, you could substitute spatial understanding or anything you like. But if you simply take a quick look at yourself looking and remember that you are an apparatus, then it becomes rather delightful and dangerous to remember what you are, how limited you are, in fact, and quite simply if you can steer a sufficiently agile course you may be able to see yourself coming, you may be able to see the back of your own head. I suppose I have this sort of objective in general. Insofar as the language will in the end defeat you, this seems to me a very honourable thing to do, to try to see what is outside the range of vision, to try to break or to catch time or the limits of the perceptive field at its tricks in limiting consciousness of the world. And make it fall flat on its own face occasionally.

JR: Another consideration with regard to this matter of representation of experience is that of experimentation. The different manners of construction and presentation in *City*, *The Ship's Orchestra*, *The Cut Pages* (and the other pieces in that book), and your use of sequences in *Matrix*—does this approach present a variety of forms to you, each of which more accurately than another form gets at or develops your material, or is it instead a more consciously experimental attitude?

RF: I very rarely do a formal experiment for form's sake. If I do I get tired of it. I get caught into a rather simple logic and if it doesn't produce sensation it's no good.

JR: By experimenting I meant (maybe it's the wrong word) the method of going about making *The Cut Pages* where you say not knowing where the next meal is coming from.

RF: No, it's not an experiment, in that I'm not seeing whether a method will work; it's methodical in the same way that trying to write a five act tragedy is methodical, or a Feydeau farce: I know what it's going to do. I'm not experimenting. I know what it's going to do as well as I would know if I were writing a Petrarchan sonnet. It just happens to be a method, and it could be called experimental only superficially in that it may well be a method which nobody's used before, if for instance I had taken the Robbe-Grillet *Snapshots* and said I'll see what happens when I use that method, because my sensibility and my life are different from his, but I would use exactly that method, that WOULD be experimental even though he had previously used the form. I would call it experimental if I wrote sonnets, in fact. But not if I use a self-branching, self-proliferating form.

JR: Do you find, then, that your use of different approaches which are self-propagating in that sense comes with the material? In other words, that it's an internally developed form, that for example in *City* the juxtaposition of poems and prose passages,—whether there's any sort of planned or controlled composition of that or whether it's just an arrangement?

RF: You have to distinguish between *City* and the other things. *The Ship's Orchestra* and *The Cut Pages* are composed works, they stand as they were composed, and if you'd seen them before they were finished you would have found them as they are (except the closing pages, which were unwritten), unaltered, and they were composed as they stand. *City* and some of the other prose pieces in *Cut Pages*—those are assemblages, they're albums. And *City* is carved from half a dozen notebooks, poems written in various towns or about various towns or no town at all. In fact it was Michael Shayer's idea that the sort of perceptual attentions given to urban things could make a work on its own. I'd been, part of the time, writing a rather pretentious pseudo-novel. I admit I was interested in the idea of a prose diary, and kept things like that. I was interested in Rilke's writings about Paris, Kafka's journals, Cocteau's things like *Opium*, and so I got the makings of it there. But the idea of that particular thing was not compositional it was editorial. Nowadays I tend to want to do a thing compositionally. I'm not too interested in book making, in how a book is assembled.

ME: For a large shift of attention: do you feel that a poet's relationship to the world is an organic relationship or a fairly artificial relationship, as a maker of poems? Do you feel he fulfils a need that is in place in the world as an organism and that works to contribute to that?

RF: If you've got a language which is not TOTALLY coded and regulated you are going to get poets because of the sheer accidents that are inherent in language systems. You're going to get language-play, as children learn their own languages; you're going to get language-play as people read shop signs, find language going mad, misbehaving in various ways. This area of language interests me very much, the inadvertent messages that come out of language, and that leak out of purposive language. You're always going to have poetry there. The rest is cultural, it depends entirely on whether anybody wants to make cultural use of unregulated language, or whether anybody wants to make language behave unregulatedly. As for the poet, or poets, no difference from any artists, for me, or no difference for that matter from a clown or debutantes and so on. Or what? He's a man who can make his activity visible. I'm not interested that a poet should have a very particular or very excellent achievement or should be any kind of intellectual hero. The interesting thing is that, with society shaped in particular ways, some people are going to be able to make their private activity, their inconsequential activity, visible in particular ways that are useful, and that is a stimulus. It feeds back into the systems, if it can be got into the systems, if it can be got to other people and it fertilises, I think. And this is very important indeed. I don't think to be a poet is decorative or merely personal.

ME: In *City* you write, 'I want to believe in a single world' and later on you say, 'what is strange is that I feel no stress, no grating comfort among the confusion, no loss, only a belief that I should not be here.' And later on in the same passage you write, 'I cannot enter that countryside; nor can I escape it. I cannot join together the mild wind and the shallow ditches, I cannot lay the light across the world and then watch it slide away. Each thought is at once translucent and icily capricious'. And I just wondered if this indicates, for you, a sort of sensibility that there is a general disruptedness about the world, a disengagement of things, where things, physical things, really lie beyond the intercourse of human activity and are like distant gods?

RF: It ties in a little bit with the bit from 'The Five Morning Poems' that you offered a little while ago. That's, again, a moment I find it hard to get back to. You know, it's fourteen years since I wrote it. And I find it dramatised in the person of the 'I' more than I can see it needed dramatising and certainly more than I'd want to dramatise it now. You see, the 'I' there speaks as if afflicted in his sensibilities and his self by this sensation. I would tend to enjoy it now, just to watch that, I wouldn't care whether I had to stay or go. It's one of the sensations that can happen to you, just as a sensation of being in a quite womb-like jam-tart and custard comfort could happen to you, and you may know why or you may not know why. If I can criticise my own work, which I'm sure I can't, that guy is wedging himself into a Byronic posture where he's forced to keep his eyelids open to that particular kind of sensation and hasn't got the discontinuous self which I would claim to live according to now, and to have portrayed in later writing.

JR: One last question. In *The Cut Pages* there's a very interesting line, I think: 'There is no process. There are many changes'. And this has attracted me considerably as a sort of turnstile for your work. I mean, taking off from that line, you seem to approach poetry as being more space-oriented than time-oriented. In other words, given the absence of a time-flow that keeps rushing away with essential insight and significance, do you think it's possible that a poet actually can hope to get to some of the essential material of his concerns? Do you feel bothered or plagued by any sort of temporal boundaries?

RF: Do you mean in life, or in terms of writing?

JR: I mean that somehow a poet trying to focus his attentions on something finds that he never can because time is shifting it out of his reach before he really can focus. And it's struck me in relation to that line, 'There is no process. There are many changes,' that if this is really true or if you believe this, then conceivably you believe it's possible for a poet to really get to the essential material that he's concerned with.

RF: If you have got your attention, and this is what you HAVE got, it is up to you to make a world to which you can attend. This is a tautology, but that's where it's at. If you decide to accept history—well, if it gives you a kick to be carried along screaming, that is your privilege. If you don't want to be carried along by your own invention, or the invention you accept, then you use some other invention. You use your attention to get, to construct something, comma, which will enable you to see. That is the beginning of a very long conversation which we can't have today, because it opens up the whole thing about what do you do when they come and beat the shit out of you with a rubber truncheon for ten minutes by the clock? Do you accept the ten minutes or not? And you'd have to go into a much more mystical or metaphysical interpretation of the whole matter. But I don't want to take it in terms of extremes. I'm talking about the way in which, in the life circumstances I have, I can use attention. And I don't feel obliged to use a large historical myth or awareness. I feel it important, if you like, to dig in outside the time flux or without regard to it, but to keep my attention in working order and not have it demoralised, I think. That would be it, that would be the sort of rationale of that I'd give.

JR: So the final thing relating to this—it's occurred to us that *The Ship's Orchestra*, *The Cut Pages*, most of *City* and *Matrix*, are unmodulated. That is, in contrast to many of the poems in *Collected Poems*, your work generally doesn't rely on highs and lows, or peaks and climactic points, any sort of catharsis or even often peaks of understanding. Instead, your work (and I think this becomes increasingly clear with re-reading) moves along on a level at which each part, each detail, is just as important as any other. And I just wondered if you agreed with this, and if this was related to the spatial/temporal distinction?

RF: I don't know if I can make that relation, but it is enormously important to me that there shall be a levelling, that there is a levelling in language – I'm not in the least concerned whether it's up or down, but the shape of the field so that anything can be picked on to give a message. Any THING, you know—the back of the knee of the man who wasn't known to be there at the time of the event which didn't happen. THAT may hold the message. And you've just got to go around looking at people's trouser legs or on the back of people's knees. You must do this. This is the child's eye view; when you're a child what you see is the backs of people's knees. You read the world in this way. You're a dog or a cat or a hedgehog. This is what I mean by subversion. Otherwise you hear the rubbish that's being talked over the top; that is ideological. This applies to the physical world, it applies to language, it applies to the art work. There's a very simple egalitarianism here, but it isn't simplistic when you get down to it, because this is the way in which things are shaken out. If I wanted to carry on into the time/space thing, you would go through people who have been much more theoretical about this like John Cage, who will have a shake-up of codes into random things and into the inconsequential. I'm not very interested in that. Theoretically I'll be willing to sit and wait for years and years for the data

71

which satisfies my theory to come out; to scramble the perceptive field. But I AM more pragmatic, I AM more driven by the sort of daffy and hourly rhythms of physical appetite and physical attention span. And given a token upset of the field, I'm interested in what I can show quite quickly.

The Seventies: from *Matrix* to *The Thing About Joe Sullivan*

Peter Robinson: You've written a number of satires (one was 'The Making of the Book') on the literary swim. Do you feel some bitterness about its way of operating?

RF: I'm a cynic in many ways, and I've just seen over the years people behaving in what to me are extraordinarily predictable patterns, people of great power, people of great intelligence digging in once they feel comfortable, and establishing a position which says things are getting a bit out of hand, let's stiffen up and give it a bit of stick. In the times I was writing some of those satires, it was the reviewing line which was 'The Group'. Again, I don't speak personally. It just seems a foolish rigour, a misplaced rigour. The rigour should be used elsewhere, and to use it socially and to make naïve assumptions about the line of verse having a magical effect upon the welfare of the commonwealth, and to say 'If we don't watch out, the edifice will crumble and there'll be blood in the gutter and wogs in the street'...

PR: That rules out Ezra Pound, then?

RF: Any bully boy thing is out for me, whether it's an atavistic bully boy, or a nostalgic one, or an academic one, or one that comes out of modernism. You can have bully boys in that just as well. I prefer heterodoxy, because it's got to be subversive.

PR: Are you conscious of making real space internalised in some work, or, as in the 'Handsworth Liberties' (which you have introduced as arising from involuntary memory), externalising an internal imagery? What is the relationship between mental space in that work, and real space—as in 'The Memorial Fountain', where a poet figure is placed against the scene?

RF: 'The Memorial Fountain' is a thing where there is a puzzle. The senses are meant to be alert and verbalising as hard as they can go, but the whole set-up is such that the senses and the mind are being presented with what appears to be an insuperable problem, and the problem is technical. It's not moral. It's a mock meditation on external space poem, a mock Gray's 'Elegy' or a 'Westminster Bridge', the *paysage moralisé*, the simple meditative man in landscape. I do a very crude thing. I put a man in a landscape and if you walk seriously three steps into the job of describing the landscape, and then work out a technique appropriate for describing the man as he finally attempts the landscape, then problems and ironies arise thick and fast.

The 'Handsworth Liberties' are almost the other way round. They are attempts to repel the invasions of landscape. I do regard this as a peculiarity of mine. I've asked plenty of people whether they suffer from this hallucination and nobody really does. It must be a crossed wire from childhood. It's probably in some textbook or other. When I was a good Freudian I thought they were all screen memories for something the mind couldn't tolerate, a sexual or insecurity thing, but there's so much of it and it's so apparently irrelevant. The 'Handsworth Liberties' do more than one thing and how I compose them is not the whole answer to how they are capable of working. I'm capable of being invaded by visual landscape, though I love visible landscape.

PR: Although there's interior memory, there is an illusion in the poems of real space. I wonder if you have transformed it into the illusion of real space?

RF: This is what I do. Here am I and into me has come, Trojan Horse fashion, something that is ineluctable, fixed, recurrent, a little chirping landscape that is visual. What I do is to dissolve its reality. (This is not in the poem.) And the poem I write is the portrait of a mind, and the senses of the self, a sense of the world, which is responding to a landscape in such a way that the landscape doesn't quite have a chance to congeal. I dramatise. I deprive the landscape of a painter's vocabulary, where I'll say 'Several miles off, there is a little row of red roofs, and in the middle distance is this and that...' In a fairly gentle way I'm dramatising the landscape to put dynamic lines in, so that there are certain imperatives—in fact, to energise, to potentiate it. I don't want a dramatically hortatory thing, but simply to give a place where, as I say in one of the poems, 'Something has to happen here'—where I'm identifying the place almost as if it were a battlefield, as if the thing you thought about most was that there was movement through it, that it was a point where the mind was conscious of change, motion.

PR: Is the sense data that makes up the poem consciously transformed into language, or does it arise as articulable units?

RF: I'm not a spontaneous singer. I make sure when doing work of this kind that isn't discursive, by travelling light, that I have a medium which I have a feel for. *The Ship's Orchestra*, which is a bit dense for what I do now, was written in writing units—and you can see the length of them, two words, four to five lines of prose, occasionally a paragraph. It's quite simply beginning and then having the feel of the line, just as if you were drawing a line, until it

73

ceased to be genuine, became fraudulent and just kept going by being inflated. I learnt to be honest with myself about the time I wrote *The Ship's Orchestra* and the 'Interiors with Various Figures', and to drop the line when it felt fraudulent. Starting to write, in my ignorance, I taught myself to do all kinds of continuity structures with rhythm. I taught myself to go on like Wallace Stevens, or to carry on tramping like Yeats. It was a pleasant moment when I could abandon metre, about which I do know something, and write a-metrical language, which in those days always had to be called prose. It's as recent as that.

I know my wind is very short. There are types of ideas which need a lot of relative clauses. I don't like them for the job we're talking about. In fact, I write something with the style of *The Sun Also Rises*. Don't expect me to claim lineage from Hemingway, but look at those things and you'll see what I mean: that particular pared-back stuff for a very short thing which doesn't make an emotional venture and doesn't compare one mode of thinking with another. I suppose I took it from the more inward-looking things in Olson's essay on Projective Verse. I keep a short string and don't use many complex sentences, which doesn't mean I am an Imagist, but I avoid long structures and, armed with that, I do the neatest job I can on complex material. So what I do is keep a minimal technique, partly because it's the one I want for the purpose, and partly because if I didn't I would overwrite dreadfully. I've got a collection of poems which have never been collected from early years, which nobody has ever published...

PR: Do you see the job of transforming visual sensations into the language of a poem by verbal manifestation as different from the use of talk in a poem, talk as in some of Ed Dorn's work, for example?

RF: Some of Ed Dorn's work is very much like that, and the work you are talking about probably also has a fair degree of consistent self-presentation. If you met Ed Dorn you would expect him to answer for his own poem in his own person, and you wouldn't automatically say that the self in the poem was different from the self walking around. For me, all that I would say is that I'm quite happy that any sort of discourse or language should find its way into a poem. I'm not, as it happens, very interested in developed characterisation, stories. In the thing about translating visual images, I know I have a lot of strong visual images. I'm always rather amazed and feel a bit pained when people say my imagery is only or predominantly visual. Sometimes I discuss the strength of visual imagery, such as in 'The Least', or 'A Poem Not a Picture', or 'The Memorial Fountain' where I'm dealing with the look of things.

I rather think that there is a reasonable quota of aural and olfactory imagery. I use quite a lot of olfactory imagery: there are a fair number of stinks and smells. I know that. I know when I'm putting them in, because they're very hard to handle. They're imprecise. You can't proliferate them. The vocabulary for smells is very crude and limited, and you just sound like a barbecue advert, sort of 'woodsmoke, armpits, honey'—a very poor vocabulary. But I use it, and I know when I'm using it, and I won't be told it isn't there; and, if I want to take a defensive position, I think people notice visual imagery because it's rather well done. I do it so they can see. I also omit other sorts of discourse, that you get in ordinary poetry, because it distracts attention from the visual. I write, I suppose, much more an English version of Robbe-Grillet, who is minute about visual detail but blank about morality, and I am—for an Englishman—very much that way.

PR: But the visual seems the most insistent?

RF: Yes, it is; I'm very conscious of it.

PR: When you talk about potentiating the landscape, does this mean that you feel no anxiety about accrediting predication to objects that don't appear to move?

RF: I know just what you mean about a language for objects. The thing is de-energised by the way language caters for it unless we do something very precious like saying 'The chairs were chairing' or some twee thing.

PR: At the beginning of 'Seven Attempted Moves' you have a wall that flowers, and it produces a kind of surrealist effect just by giving the object a verb.

RF: It's got to move. I could claim to have written it in the consciousness of your recent question. What I do in that poem is to give the stranger no comfort like in the opening passage of a Flaubert novel: 'A little way outside the village of so and so, there is a particularly interesting wall.' It is as follows, and so on. So you have a wall, and 'On a fine summer evening, you could see her...' I'm not doing that at all. I start with a colour: 'If the night were not so dark / this would be seen / Deep red, / the last red before black' or something of this sort. Then I don't say 'There's a wall'. I say 'Beside the soft earth steps'—which is dislocative, a challenge. Steps are occasionally made out of earth, but not for long. The wall, whatever it is, 'breathes and / flowers / and breathes'. There, if it works, I'm directing anybody reading the thing to understand that they must be working from a vocabulary of inward experience, and that they are in a world free of the reality principle.

PR: But it does have an air of real space about it?

RF: Space is part of our mental life. We sit here merrily thinking we know all about the relativity of spatial dimensions, but I take it we may not. I do assume that three-dimensional space looks the same to those I'm talking to as it does to me, especially when we're passing things to each other, because our language is one which coarsens it. We haven't a language for space-time. We haven't a four-dimensional language at all. I suppose a lot of what we're talking about here is my perhaps rather small but insistent attempt to assume that a four-dimensional perception is somehow necessary for us to have...the moral at last!

Robert Sheppard: Near the end of your recently published Oxford University Press *Poems 1955-1980* there occurs the poem 'Wonders of Obligation', in which I detect a distinct change of tone in your work. You spoke—in 1973 in one of the two interviews that you did—of the possibility of retreating permanently from the topographical and narrative and yet here you seem to be confronting these head on. In earlier texts you'd written of living by the eye and there is a character in 'Seven Attempted Moves' who has 'respect for neither side/just for things happening'. The detachment is clear. Although in 'Wonders of Obligation' you still argue, 'The things we make up out of language / Turn into common property', you do add emphatically, 'To feel responsible / If I put my poor footprint back in'. I was curious about your changing sense of 'responsibility.'

RF: I haven't got a coherent theoretically expressible point of view there, it's just that I feel able to use something like a self. Put it this way: I feel that the persona, the thing called 'I' in that poem, is more accessible for me to use in a piece of writing than it used to be.

RS: Why's that?

RF: Age; getting knocked about! There's a very elaborate answer, in fact. It's something to do with the fact that the sort of sensibility I had in the *City* period, through the block which followed and, at a fair remove to the late sixties—it was a very phobic personality. *City*, for instance, is very much bits that are left from a very hairy epic novel-cum-poem. And if you look at the self-structures or the narratives—the buried narrative—or the quasi-dramatic situations in the older work there is nearly always a myth of a person who leaves life.

RS: An observer.

RF: May not even observe. It may be lost or shut away, a completely lost man, a person who is turned to stone, for instance. It doesn't feature in many of the published works but it features in a lot of the ones that got discarded: the idea of the person becoming a statue, becoming reified. This was very much part of the sensibility. It isn't any more. It was a biographical stage—of how I was in a very fixed or tragic mode. I've been working through a lot of the old notebooks lately. What I've found is that I'm amazed at the amount of rigidity and removal there is in the whole of the work I was writing at that time and publishing only the drier bits. I think that whatever I saw, whatever I got out, in the old work about twenty years ago, was got at that price, out of quite a neurotic personality, through to about 1973 when I got unblocked, and I was writing rather quickly the work that's in *Joe Sullivan*, I was not particularly yet occupied with appearing in the work, standing up and being counted or whatever—being 'responsible' if you like. But I was just running a lot of perceptual games in those, while they were there. In later things I felt, I can only say, a bit more robust. There isn't a theoretical change. I would probably have written the way I'm writing now twenty years earlier if I'd as robust a self. But I was not. I was timid and retired, and a somewhat phobic person.

RS: Coming back to 'Wonders of Obligation', when did you write it?

RF: It's three years ago this summer.

RS: There is very little of your characteristic 'making strange' in 'Wonders of Obligation'. You've spoken of Birmingham as being like a science-fiction empire, and when I wrote about it I hardly ever called it by its name, which is what you said on the radio. In 'Wonders of Obligation' you return to the bombing raids of your most famous but, as you've also said, most 'atypical' poem, 'The Entertainment of War'; and you write about the 'mass graves for the poor of Birmingham / the people of Birmingham / the working people of Birmingham', hammering home its name. Did formalism—your alienation techniques—finally become too alienating? Did you step back from that in that piece—consciously?

RF: Again, by gut-feeling. My formalism also arises from whatever the equivalent is, for formalists, of gut-feeling! It's instinctive, the formalism—I know just what you mean—the perceptual games and so forth, and the Beckett, Kafka or whatever queries about ... all the ontology stuff. 'A Poem Not a Picture' is exactly that.

RS: The 'scratch ontology.'

RF: Yes. For me that isn't programmatic there. The way I move from one thing to another is very much by blind appetite, and what I would say is that I hate to repeat; I hate to imitate myself or do another one in my usual manner because that doesn't interest me at all. I don't like to display. And for me a puzzle is a puzzle. And if I've solved it I don't want to ask it again. I may write the same puzzle because I've forgotten that I've already solved it. But normally I would say that what would be happening about the time of 'Wonders' is that I didn't feel the pressure of the perceptual games. And I wouldn't go so far as to say that I felt the pressure of saying, 'I must speak out; I must speak roundly,' but it gave me pleasure to do so. (Laughter.) There's a change from the *City* work in that I very carefully didn't use a named Birmingham at that point, partly because I was doing something a bit like the work of a novelist who just gives himself the ordinary license of changing Oxford, Mississippi into Jefferson or Dorchester into Casterbridge, the ordinary license of avoiding the entailments of documentary realism, which would be very heavy for me because I've got photographic optical memory. I have to make the city strange in order to be able to move my mind in it at all. Otherwise I would be just be left with super-realism, which would drive me screaming mad because I really can remember window-frames and bricks and things.

So there isn't a change in programme. It's just a matter of what I can do. If I'd been writing a long novel about the city I would have had to invent names for it. Durrell, who I have to admit was an influence at the time, although I'm amazed to think of it now, he would continually talk about the Old Poet. Everybody knew he was talking about Cavafy. But he would choose not to name him so that he wouldn't be lumbered by everything that was true about Cavafy. I was ducking out in that way just to give myself room to move. But if I've got room to move in the 'Wonders' I take it that I've got other sorts of room to move. I can't quite describe what they are. So I don't need to use the evasions. I don't need to avoid mentioning them by name.

RS: But it also seems that you're very insistently naming it in that passage. And responding perhaps to the earlier work, I thought.

RF: I don't think I thought I was. But I wouldn't deny that I was! (Laughter.) I don't think I thought of it that way.

I was just soap-boxing a bit. And feeling more like doing it. In the old days I would look with wonderment at a poet who could name names. You know *Briggflatts*! Bunting actually names a river and will say that 'this little counter— I've called it Rawthey—that will answer to what another person might see who went to that place.' I had no such confidence at one time. There are one or two things, like the 'Glenthorne Poems' which was from some circumstances and some experience that I wasn't in two minds about. And I could handle it. And I wanted to use names. To me that was a great freedom. I think it will probably occupy me in the future, to wonder what it is about the naming of a name that has had difficulties for me.

RS: You've just reminded me of a poem, a Louis MacNeice poem, called 'Birmingham', a very early one.

RF: 'Smoke from this train-gulf hid by hoardings blunders upward...'. I learnt it by heart at school.

RS: Yeah? What do you think of it?

RF: I've no idea what I think of it ! it's still too close to me. It was one of the three or four things that had ever been written about Birmingham, to my knowledge.

RS: In *City* you say, 'Most of it has never been see'.

RF: I knew perfectly well it had been seen by Auden, with whom I have this very remote family connection, and by MacNeice, and it had been seen by Walter Allen. He wrote some novels about Birmingham in which he'd done all these games of calling it 'The City' and so forth in the 1930s. He was born in about 1911 a few miles from where I was born. I read these novels from a local library when I was a student and I was quite excited to realise that anybody who had seen the place could actually write about it. And I think bits of Auden, bits of MacNeice, bits of Allen. I can understand Allen's attitude reasonably well. I didn't know when I was young what Auden's nature was at all. I didn't know what kind of sensibility he had with relation to this material. I was just excited by the naming that he did, even though it didn't look in the least bit like what I saw when I looked. I didn't know at the time the degree to which MacNeice was contemptuous of Birmingham and was just doing his thing about it. I was so amazed that anybody could write and live in the city and use anything. The MacNeice poem: it's a terribly swanky poem, and nothing like me. But there are one or two things. There's a very good Birmingham industrial sunset, or Middlesbrough or Stockport industrial sunset—well worth doing. That turned me on. I lived with those things.

RS: It's also loaded with classical allusion I seem to remember as well.

RF: 'The Vulcan's Forges'. It was a poem we had to have the teacher translate: 'crême-de-menthe' turned into 'bull's blood' ! We all drank Corona pop !

RS: In earlier statements you've dodged ...

RF: [Laughter.] And now I've got to stop dodging!

RS: ... questions of political affiliation or political implications for your work.

RF: I haven't dodged them all that much.

RS: I thought maybe you were dodging at times some of the things Donald Davie wrote about your work in *Thomas Hardy and British Poetry*.

RF: I wasn't aware that he'd exactly written about my work in that book!

RS: Whether you were dodging his annexations of you for social democratic writing about industrial landscapes, etc ... etc ...

RF: I know what you mean, if we use the words 'social democratic' in their old sense. What I resist, in that sort of thing, is the connotation of what is for me bourgeois – the social democratic outlook of bourgeois guardianship. I mean the Richard Hoggart view. I don't know these people well—I don't know a lot of what they think—but I suppose I would depart from Davie, not through any advance position, but just through shirking the issue: the sort of belief, I think, [he would have] in the mid-sixties and leading up to the writing of that book: that there was an arena of informed debate about the true nature of British culture and that it might be found in the *New Statesman* or an *Encounter* article: wherever George Steiner might be, or wherever Donald Davie might be. In later years there might be *PN Review*—taking a more embattled, disappointed and consequently a more right-wing view—in a disappointed belief in benign, informed values; Arnold-through-Leavis-through-Raymond Williams. I'm deeply sceptical about that point of view and about that view of social structure. Which doesn't mean that you will find me a Marxist in any formal sense or an anarchist in any formal sense, but on the whole you'll find me to the left—or further out—of those people. Not so much in terms of any programme but in terms of distrust of elites and those who constitute them. And I believe that the British forum of articulate culture-bearers is a self-deluding group.

RS: Recently, in answer to my own questionnaire, you wrote, 'I believe all my poetry to be didactic'. And I was very intrigued and, I think, heartened to hear you say, on that BBC programme *The Living Poet*, that the political content of your work resides in its perceptual counters, the reminders of the complexity of the perceptual mechanisms that show us the world.

RF: I thought they were going to leave that bit out!

RS: How is that political, for you?

RF: It's political in the sense that—and this is the didacticism I suppose—the world is made particularly in its social manifestations, in its economics, by mental models. That's not an unfamiliar view. And it's probably in Blake, who's about as near to the political position that I have as anybody. The human mind makes the world. The examination of this organism that makes the world is of paramount interest. If we do not know how our minds work, and how our appetites work, and how our senses and our rationalisations are interactive, and consequently can go on kidding ourselves about the shapes we make about the differences between sex and murder, money and death—unless we know that, we're very poorly equipped to interpret the forms by which we live, i.e. the political dimension of the world. All I ask for is to have the imagination regarded—this sounds like Williams I suppose—as politicised because the imagination will make the world. And if it isn't my imagination, it's Margaret Thatcher's imagination. She is a deeply imaginative woman. Rhodes Boyson is a deeply imaginative man. They have visions of the world. They have interpretations, rationalisations. I speak of two quite mild examples. It may be naive, but that's the link for me. I am, if anything, a specialist in those processes. I work very largely by introspection anyway, rather than by uttering any generalisations about how we are. I believe, with a sort of horse-sense, that how I say I am holds good for quite a number of processes which take place in other people, otherwise I wouldn't have any readers at all. And I believe that I am also describing the experience of many people who, for various cultural reasons, don't read me. just as there are many people who are in the same boat with regard to Bill Burroughs; he describes many people's experience. Nabokov—very strong. They tell us a great deal about how we create streets, houses, workhouses, redundancy schemes, welfare, war. That's all. And I specialise in the inner selves.

I'm very conscious of needing to assure myself that that is what I've done, and to clarify to myself what it is that I've done, and to proceed to work that makes the connection explicit. Because I find it very surprising that people will look at my work as if it was pure aestheticism or look at it as without moral dimension at all. It's a bit strange to me though I know that if I look at it from one angle myself, it is.

But I find it puzzling in many of the hard-working, but more mainstream, reviews of the Oxford book to find intelligent people having to work hard to determine any slant or tenor in my work or to regard it as in any way politicised or socialised. Interestingly enough I was working with Adrian Mitchell, who is obviously verbally and stylistically an extremely different animal from me, and whose texts are utterly different phenomena: I said, drily, in the course of a reading, how his messages were very clear while whatever political element was in my poems was apparently too obscure to see. And he said, 'That's nonsense. Your politics are absolutely apparent to anybody who knows what they might be. One or another form of anarchism.'

RS: You've said before that you don't really think of a reader. Are you now aware of the reader?

RF: Yes.

RS: Has that changed since the Oxford book?

RF: No. This has been very, very gradual. I stopped being able to write when I found anybody was reading me. That was really a terrible shock. Then with the passage of time, quite childishly, it helped to get a bit of praise. I don't set a huge amount of store by praise but I quite like to be left in no doubt— from the sort of consumer-test with the odd review and so forth—the stuff is apparently of use, or that if it's a knife it cuts, or if it's an engine it runs. I'd be worried if the work seemed a personal dig for ego-recognition. It's got to work as poetry. So that's been consolidating. I suppose, in more recent years, I've got used to turning up at readings and so forth and seeing people receive the work. That makes a difference. I can imagine a type of reader and I've met enough people who've read enough of the work: quite a few people who've read three or four poems, something like that. My penetration to anything more than a pretty specialised public of other poets, or of poet/scholars like yourself, is very small and it rests entirely upon about three funny poems and two or three topographical ones.

RS: I'm surprised at that. I thought maybe the Oxford book would have made some difference because earlier you've spoken of having an audience that was more or less a small network. I thought maybe that might have changed recently.

RF: It's probably the case that more people are treating some of the stuff as slow reading matter, which is what I want. But so far as readings are concerned, I like to turn out on readings to see what happens. I would think that I get booked to do readings—other than places like this and one or two London readings, or Colpitts—very largely because of a very small number of atypical poems. The main 'lab-work', which you do, which I do, you and I do, is not particularly noticed. But what was interesting about the reviews of the Oxford book—and I include what I call the mainstream reviews in things like *Quarto* and *TLS*—is that they just weigh in and do a quite straightforward job, without talking about who my friends are. Or why I'm not like Philip Larkin and things of this extraordinary sort. But I was interested at the number of people who, with their own visible sort of academic training, a lot of people in their thirties, part of a certain generation, were able to say, 'Ah ha, I'm puzzled by certain factors in this, by certain things that appear to be paradoxical, such as this man appears to read Americans and be English and doesn't seem to speak like a cowboy,' and that persuades me that the work is readable to a careful reader. It makes me feel rather less arid.
    Indeed, what I like—why I'm interested in what I do—is largely for the desire to be lyrical, despite all the evidence. The 'Wonders' has got some lyric in it. And I sort of enjoy it in a quite hammy fashion: all that stuff about the rain and the dark night. It's the Tennysonian streak in many ways, you know. And I'd used my data and Tennyson's music. And I'm quite happy with that.

RS: Yes, you've spoken about trying to get the 'meatier' bits of poetry into more radical formal circumstances in an interview.

RF: I've forgotten that!

RS: A different question again. Lineation in your poetry seems peculiarly linked to 'linearity of concepts', to the movement of thought and sensation. There's one comment you made in an interview which I've never been able to make head or tail of and that is: 'Wittgenstein's *Tractatus* was a very splendid sort of stylistic influence... and I paid far more attention to the *Tractatus* as a mode of lineation... than to any poet'. Can you help me out on that?

RF: Yeah! You know how he writes it: the idea of a proposition which is about to hold firm and then to be expanded on or qualified quite formally. Rather than my own earlier, and I think very crappy and half-baked, view, which was that you had a huge wobbling mass which had no structure, knew no law because it was afraid to know law in case law was just unpleasant, and kindled itself along, puffed and puffed itself. I used to write terrible iambics, the sort of stuff where—you know—the fourth line from where you are is going to rescue the line you've written by making an overall shape which casts the lifebelt out.

That's what I'm talking about: lineation possibly in a conceptual, rather than a metrical, sense. The breakthrough for me was the 'Interiors' where I was able to write in conceptual units—it doesn't sound much now but you have to remember that particularly in England everybody was writing in metre, the people who got published. Even most of the poems in *City* would be thought to be very adventurous by the tastes of the late '50s, not rhyming too much and so forth. But in the 'Interiors', particularly the short ones in the sequence, 'The Steam Crane' and 'The Billiard Table'—you know, 'Before breakfast you drew down the blind' and 'Why should I let him shave the hairs from me?'— those were a great liberation in that I was just making forms with remarks which, if written tightly, were my units. So I freed myself from fraudulent log-rolling, which was still hanging about in my ear.

It's utterly pragmatic, not theoretical, acknowledgement that I made to Wittgenstein. I was just reading the English translation and just enjoying the crack of it. I'd been a great sort of blotcher. Again, you have not been able to read—as I can!—my masterpieces like 'The Fog at Birmingham' and 'The Image' which one or two people have seen in past years and have retired ashen-faced from. They really are very manic: very hairy epics.

RS: I was wondering also whether Gael Turnbull's poems had any influence on you—I was thinking particularly of the 'Six Fancies' where he uses a 'prose' paragraph—in two senses. They seem rather close to the 'Interiors' in their paragraphic arrangement and also very close to the 'making strange' of the 'Interiors'.

RF: Gael and I: very different people, but I suspect we influence each other in funny ways as the years go by. And we've always been quite close associates in a way. It was many years before I took his work seriously, as I now do, because I was very interested in writing in a way that would carry a huge suffused weight of need and image and passion or something, which obviously is not evident in much of what I've published. That's what I wanted to do and I thought Gael's work was very thin. And it turns out that I am the one who's published the thin work, the drier or rarefied work. His 'collected works' is, in fact, quite hefty. But not a direct influence I think, except again that I was always

83

fascinated at the way in which he would use whatever form he wanted to, when I was being stuffy about what form it should be in.

RS: Why do you think he was able to do that?

RF: Two things. One was that he was extremely idealistic about poetry, which I never was, and wanted very much to be in the world of poetry, whereas I've never understood the world of poetry or felt I belonged to it. He wanted to belong to it and has been hurt by the indifference of it to him. And that's a great loss to it. Secondly he would tirelessly work on formal matters day in, day out. He would expose himself to a great deal of poetry and would set himself the standard of formal invention, and would want to invent, whereas I would still be imitative well on into my maturity in works of mine which got published as original. Very often they were the odd ones that I would be doing when I wasn't trying to write like Yeats or David Jones, or something like that. I wouldn't know what I ought not to write.

RS: I was also wondering about Gael Turnbull's 'Twenty Words, Twenty Days', that rather formalistic way of doing things. I was wondering whether that had any influence over you in the 'additive form' of *The Ship's Orchestra* and, after that, *The Cut Pages*. It only occurred to me recently that there might be that influence.

RF: Not a direct influence, but again, one of those things where there is common ground, where you know that you can work like that. The *Orchestra*—that's somewhat Wittgensteinian in a way. You couldn't quite put Wittgensteinian numbering on that—no you couldn't, but it has that spirit; it's a parody, in a way, of that. All that's missing is the relevance. (Laughter). The idea of working formal devices without being bound by your own formal commitment to it—that occurs in the 'Metamorphoses' or in the 'Interiors' which have all got a set of formal constituents, the haircut, the loose clothes, the milk bottle and using them as a painter would. I don't know how Gael came upon that way of working. We were separated by thousands of miles, really, when he wrote that one. It's all about what it is possible to do. And again, being free from readership, oddly enough, would matter then. He published that in *Poetry* in Chicago, so he had an audience for that kind of thing—which I certainly didn't. I had no access to magazines like that and never have had.

RS: Moving on to 'The Cut Pages', why did you not reprint it in *Poems 1955-1980*?

RF: It's out of scale to the rest of the writing in a way in which I don't quite understand. If you put it along with the other work it occupies an enormous amount of space for what is transacted in it. I'm not saying that it wastes space. The normal ratio of didactic event to space occupied in my work is more rapid.

And this work, I couldn't see it in a collection. I could see it better as a completely free-standing thing, preferably artistically done and certainly not a small print text, reduced in size and squashed. I thought it would probably provide an area which would seem a sort of desert within the book. And it wouldn't do its thing. It wouldn't function as I'd want it to.

RS: So it wasn't dissatisfaction with it?

RF: Oh no! I don't mind the work. I don't know the work very well. It was an exercise in freedom. But I would like to see it in a coffee-table size, you know, quite large, if anybody ever wanted to do it pretty. Not only out of interest in the text. Occasionally artists take images out of it. I would like to have it so it would work for artists.

RS: What made you write it?

RF: It was extraordinary. I'd been blocked. I got rid of the block. I absented myself from life—I had a year's sabbatical—and started off by typing up all my old unpublished work, quite a bit of which has since been published, and looking at what it was—just getting into myself. Then I wrote quite quickly 'Glenthorne Poems', I think I wrote those in a few days. I said: this year, 1970, I will write. So I wrote the 'Glenthorne Poems' taking it easy, not running into any of my old conundrums which used to block me, largely because I was trying too hard. Then 'The Cut Pages'. I just did an exercise in self-permission, assuming there was no reader, there was no critic, no monitor. I've got, as it says in the book, a journal and general notebook. I'd had a really grisly year or so of my life and had written a good deal about the grisliness of my at that point. And had really been at my wit's end. And I was feeling rather better but was still within the confines of this bound notebook. And I didn't enjoy turning the pages which had unhappy things on them to get to the blank paper, which is always a pleasant sight. So I cut the blank pages out with a razor and wrote on them—freely. The equation was quite simple: that I'd written in the earlier parts of the book what life demanded that I should attend to—heavy matters— and I did the converse in the other one. I wrote what there was no constraint upon. And worked in that way, without even 'being myself' or addressing myself to my normal concerns. That's all. I went on doing it for a certain number of pages, or a certain length of time, I've forgotten. To use that stack of paper.

RS: I often think, when I read them, of Williams's improvisations.

RF: I was thinking of *Kora in Hell*, yes. But not directly. I was thinking of it as a theme. I wrote it quite quickly. It was a period when I had several ideas. I then wrote 'Metamorphoses' and I wrote 'The Six Deliberate Acts' and was planning 'Matrix', and I wrote that when I had time. So I did all that, I'd written the 'Glenthorne Poems', 'The Cut Pages', 'Metamorphoses', and 'The Six

Deliberate Acts' within maybe two months, after being blocked for four or five years. Then I had the *Matrix* poems and wrote that when I was not busy. That was quite a bunch of things.

It was an unblocker, 'The Cut Pages', very much, an uncorking. And I still haven't gone back to it to see what is transacted. It's probably a work I'd like to rewrite parts of in a quite different form, and use the energy. Largely I think there are tracks of it that don't address themselves to any particular direction. I'm rather fascinated by what it came up with. It's very automatic.

RS: It might seem obvious to include your poetry in any collection of an English 'poetry of place'. And, as you know, the term was much used in the '70s.

RF: I believe that's the case! I walked off a platform on which it was being discussed in 1966, because I was bored with the discussion! So I didn't keep up with it after that.

RS: But would I be right in saying that—except in certain parts of *City*— your reactions to place are as much to do with memory as with topography? I am thinking particularly of 'Handsworth Liberties'.

RF: Yes. Completely. The 'place' tag is not very meaningful to me. It just happens that for reasons of timidity and inability and agoraphobia and fear of travel sickness and goodness knows what, I didn't travel. I would actually take great justification in never going anywhere from the fact that Williams took a lot out of his own spot and would conveniently ignore in my mind the fact that he spent huge amounts of time in Europe as a child and later on. But it was just phobia about travel. I remember, by 1967, to go from Birmingham to Coventry was an incredible adventure for me. I could conceal this, but I had complete travel phobia. I just happened to talk quite articulately—as people with phobias will—about things that are available within the constraints of the phobia. So I went very deeply into that and then went into it partly ideologically. But I'm in some reaction against that. I got quite a few things out of it but it was not a very intelligent position for a person who had any choice. But I hadn't a choice. There was nowhere else I could be. I was a very immobile person. If I'd lived in fifteen places in my childhood ...

RS: ...you'd have fifteen different memories.

RF: ... I'd have fifteen different memories and I'd talk about them just the same as I do. It so happens that I lived in the same house twenty three years, and slept in one or two bedrooms in twenty three years. So I've got some very consolidated memories. There's nothing programmatic about the fact that they are the same—it's purely gratuitous—which is why 'place' for me is not very good news. (Laughter.) It's interesting but once it moves into—I'm not very good at separating space-time—that odd thing of Davie's: how anybody after Einstein can separate history from geography puzzles me somewhat. I know what he's trying to do but it seems a bit stalky. I found quite simply, that having a very long memory, the place is visibly unstable, though it stays stable in itself. And to be in Birmingham now: I could only be in Birmingham as a journalist writing about what I once thought of it. I did write one piece for *Vole*. But I could only do it in terms of concepts. I couldn't use the place again.

I'm really rather puzzled by the 'place.' If I read Ed Dorn or Olson it would never occur to me to think of it as a poetry of place. Or *Paterson* for that matter. In that what seems strange to me is the poetry of no place, which is just Baedeker or tourism.

There's a different matter which is the physical fetishism of the scene: you get that in Hardy or Tennyson. And the physical fetishism of 'Mariana in the Moated Grange' is of the same order as the fetishism of some of *City*. He's writing about Somersby and I'm writing about a mythical version of where I was. But the physical fetishism of the scene of the fictive poem, that's a different matter and I don't think that's got much to do with ... the English landscape.

RS: What has it got to do with?

RF: Oh. I think it's almost certainly got to do with body-image projections: libido. I'm about to embark one of these days on a sizeable work on the bit of landscape I'm intending to go and live in: the moorland just north of where I live now, which is an incredible area about twenty miles across and ten miles wide. It's inconceivable. I know it very well but I can hold no single concept of it. It's about as big as Birmingham. It's hill country. I've got a weird thing working. It'll probably finish up looking more like *Maximus Poems* or *Paterson*, not stylistically, but it'll address itself to a tract of country in a different way from the way the Birmingham stuff was done. I don't know what it's going to be like: check it out, see if I can do it. I feel very moved to do all this because it's shifting—it is extremely concrete, and historically very stable: you can look back a couple of thousand years in the rivers. It's very much the area Peter Riley wrote about in *Lines On the Liver*—a splendid book. That's where he sits in Wirksworth on the other side of it and looks at the area with that telephone box. I know that box well! God, it takes the hair off of your head to think about that area. It's a mystery!

I find the 'place' tag is a very literal one, and I'm not a literalist.

RS: There seems to be some debate over questions of foreign influences in your work. Jed Rasula, in his interview, seems to insist upon the American connection. John Ash, in his *Atlantic Review* article, emphasises European modernist and post-modernist influence. He seems also to be locating himself as a poet in that article. Your earliest 'contacts' were Americans, weren't they? Were they influences as well, do you think?

RF: I don't think that in any actual text that I've produced there is very much direct influence by any particular American text. But I am aware that what I think is an influence may be—put it another way: influence works on various levels. I could, for instance, in some works have very clearly in my mind—explicit—the fact that I know myself to be thinking about some of the Europeans I've talked about before: Klee, Kafka, Cocteau. Or thinking about Picasso or Stravinsky, or Daumier, or Emil Nolde, often painters. Thomas Mann. And on the whole I am a little bit more likely to have been thinking of one of those people when I'm thinking of planning a particular work. I know, for instance, that the idea of being freed to write about city-matters was given a kick by a sentence that occurs—and must still be there—in Pasternak's *An Essay in Autobiography*. I would be quite likely to know that I was writing a variation on a passage in *Doctor Zhivago* or that I had consciously, in my mind a passage of text from *Safe Conduct* or the milieu of a passage of text from a Kafka 'Diary'. So in the actual business of writing I would nearly always be more able to find a European take-off point. I haven't got a clear sense of this.

At the same time, the American contacts I had had a more general influence on me, in that I acquired a sense from them of what it was like to make art in a general sense, why it was the thing you did. And you have to remember that I was exposed to jazz music for maybe ten years before. The tones and sayings and outlooks and attitudes, particularly of white mid-western jazz musicians, and the actual forms they used and the ways they had of tackling things, were very familiar to me. So to swing across to American painters, poets, was a fairly lateral thing but, on the whole, a vague one. I think I was rather aware that you could not address a piece of work as if you were an American. If you are English—and know you're English—and your ambience is that of the English-British-literary establishment and its magazines and channels; if you then play a game of pretending you're an American or behaving as if, hypothetically, you were an American addressing yourself in a piece of work, your gesture is a little odd. You might, for instance, not know that you're doing it. Lee would be a good example of somebody who has been wrongly taken to be mid-Atlantic—a 'fan' of what's American. So in the English competitive game he goes down. I think that in certain review debacles he'd suffer from exactly that. Tom Raworth suffered, like Gael, who is mid-Atlantic genetically and in all sorts of genuine ways; they suffered. Because the thing you must not do in England—unless you're a disc-jockey—is seem to be following American leads. It's making yourself vulnerable.

Whereas I think that what I found was that, without thinking more than twice about it, I would say to myself: I am on a number fifteen bus in Birmingham. I am familiar with the sensibility of Paul Klee or Kokoschka but I'm not familiar with the places they were at, but I'll play some perceptual games and I will de-Anglicise England—which seems to me absolutely essential. You can't do it in terms of America. (When I was in America I was amazed at how familiar it was from my knowledge of the English industrial Midlands.) I would do exercises in de-Anglicising England. To imagine, for instance, that you had a French education or a Swiss or a German education, Austrian education.

RS: Like those 'Chinese' paintings of the Lake District.

RF: Yeah. Exactly. Or as if you had a degree in jurisprudence at the University of Prague like Kafka and worked in a Birmingham insurance office and your degree in jurisprudence and your job meant the same thing to you in the Birmingham insurance office as it would in Prague and the same deference or the same guilt, or whatever it might be, were culturally present for you. Whereas I knew very well that there's this incredible mishmash of English indefinition. I'm not saying I was putting the boot in but I was simply—that's 'making strange' if you like—I would imagine that kind of sensibility and those sorts of determinants into what I was used to. I was reading of how Picasso was fascinated by views of England and how Buñuel had the same sort of view about the wetness of Newcastle-upon-Tyne! (Laughter.) I would take that literally and say: okay, I can't see England because of the education system. What I now know is that nearly all the reading matter I've had about what England looked like, and sounded like, and felt like, was produced by people who were products of the public school system, because that's the way you get to write books! I didn't know it until quite a late date, but it's a fact. And all sorts of gestures and so forth are built into that. I was always feeling for alternative gestures or angles in. And I would take them from European novels where you had a different education, a different social sense.

It's part of my education that I never had 'modernism' explained fully and neither did I have it disproved. And I think I said on the radio thing that it seems to me all the Big League of modernism seems so enormous in implication, far too enormous to be rolled along on peoples' careers, when new careers come along. And I strangely wanted to re-visit that and go into it and see what the hell was going on.

RS: And also inevitably to come up with something different because you lived in a different historical time.

RF: That's right. It's no time for manifestos. One thing you can't do is make manifestos about it. I'm not the sort of man to behave like Apollinaire.

The Eighties and Nineties:
From *Poems 1955-1980* to *The Dow Low Drop*

John Tranter: What's you relationship with academia? You went into academia fairly early in the piece, yet you seem to me to be the sort of poet who hasn't gone into the academic line at all. You seem to have veered away from it all through your writing life.

RF: I suppose so. I've never been conscious of there being an academic literary tradition around me in the country. I couldn't in this country say that so-and-so is a 'campus poet', in the way in which you can say this about American poets who live on campus.

JT: I think it's a very American thing, isn't it?

RF: Yes. If you can graduate in Creative Writing, and take a doctorate in it, and then get a job teaching it, that's a quite different life from anything that's available over here. There are scraps of it. There are one or two programs; very few programs for a credit, and they are minor parts of degree courses. There was a time when you could be a writer-in-residence on an Arts Council grant at a university campus, but that by English standards was regarded as far too leisurely an existence. You just officially seemed to be staying in a place of comfort. If you had that sort of job you weren't required to run credit programs. You would be seeing the odd people who wrote a bit and you'd do a reading and get some of your friends in to do a program of readings. Funds for that sort of a thing in this country nowadays tend to be attached to all sorts of community activity programs and they're out of academia almost completely, I think.

JT: So what's the work you've done in universities?

RF: I was just an ordinary literature teacher. I worked in colleges for a long time. We have—or we had—a sort of intermediate higher education institution, which was essentially for training teachers. And in those days they were of a more modest grade than universities. People didn't need to be so well qualified to get in. I quite enjoyed working at a couple of those. For quite a lot of the time I was teaching 'method' rather than teaching 'literature', and in fact I ducked out from teaching literature straight, as much as I could. I taught all sorts of things, like story-telling skills, and children's literature, and how to control a class, and things of this sort, having been a school-teacher for a time. And I didn't particularly want to have to handle the idea of being half in criticism, scholarship; and I rather enjoyed teaching in institutions where you could in fact set quite a fast pace of work—particularly with adult students, with whom I worked for ten or twelve years—with a complete freedom of curriculum. If I wanted to teach Catullus in translation and Dostoyevsky in translation—what I could read, not having the languages—I could teach that. Whereas in university programs, they tend to be rather more hidebound, you know, English literature written in English for the English was basically what you had to do. That was the case twenty or thirty years ago. It loosened up.

When I went to teach in a university in the end, I carefully joined an American Studies department and taught in an American Studies program, so as to teach literature which was of interest [to me]. I just taught modern literature, nineteenth and twentieth century literature, fiction and poetry. I did that really so as not to get caught up in the rather head-cracking debates about how to teach English literature as such. You know, you get into the debates about how much theory there should be, how much structuralism there should be, how much Marxism there should be. Those are truly academic debates. I wasn't too bothered with them.

JT: They're political debates too, debates about who has the power and who doesn't, and who controls the latest fashion and who doesn't.

RF: They all seem to me to be reductive. In the long run they turn out to be dedicated to honing the curriculum down and down and down to a smaller and smaller canon which will have certain sharp socio-political edges. I'm not interested in that.

JT: I talked to Frank Kermode a bit about that when he was in Australia recently. He went through a very rough time at Cambridge going through exactly that kind of argument.

RF: He would indeed.

JT: Trying to loosen things up a bit, I think, and introduce new ideas, and of course that's hard to do in an older university. Old is old, too. That goes back hundreds and hundreds of years. You have a weight of tradition to push against there which can be quite frustrating.

RF: And all those debates to do with academic fashion, they're conducted with what is apparently a very high moral purpose, but they're very introverted debates, and to my way of thinking they come down to matters of intellectual style rather than of cultural substance, or anything which has got an active muscle in it.

JT: The art critic Peter Schjeldahl argued a few years ago in Australia [in his keynote address to the Adelaide Festival Artists' Week in February 1986] that fashion and style are very good things because they help to focus the spotlight of attention on what's the newest and the best and the most energetic work being done in any particular field, and they save you the impossible task of having to read literally everything, which no one can do.

RF: Oh yes ... I take that ... ah, I would probably have taken it more when I was younger. The way I get to feel as I grow older and see a few more cycles go around—and I'm fairly slow at catching fashions and knowing what's going on, and people never tell me anything—probably I'm the sort of person who manages not to be told things—but as I see the cycles go around, I get a bit spaced out. I sit back and ... try to think on eternity, and what is substantial and what is historically important over a long period. I don't tend to get very much disturbed or very much excited by what seems to be going on this minute. I don't get too much from it.

JT: You've just had three books out in the last few years from Oxford University Press, which seems like a blast of fashionability.

RF: You get remarks on some books that say 'This book is made from recycled paper.' My books maybe ought to have a warning saying 'This book is made from recycled books.' In fact the Oxford *Collected* of 1980 was almost entirely composed of most of four Fulcrum books, plus one Carcanet book. Then *A Furnace*, which was a separate book, and is a single free-standing work, was almost all I've published during the eighties. And the *Poems 1955-1987* is a recycling of the 1980 *Collected*, with ten or twenty pages added. So some of the contents of these books are having their third and fourth and fifth time around. It all comes from the fact that the first verse collection I did with Fulcrum was called *Collected Poems*, which was my first collection of poems. And I also thought it was going to be my last, because I was in the block, and I wasn't expecting to write any more poems. So I have this habit of 'collecting' as I go. So some of these poems have been 'collected' quite a few times.

JT: That's what writers used to do a hundred years ago, isn't it? They'd bring out a book, then the next edition would have a few more poems, and they'd go on adding to the one book. Each book they brought out was a more complete version of their work. So that as their lives went along, the book grew with them, as it were.

RF: Well, yes. That's quite congenial to me. It's probably why I publish with Oxford, who have done a few books of that sort. I don't write much, you see. Also a lot of what I do write is an attempt to make sense, or make art, or make form of what were inchoate experiences some while ago. Or even inchoate writings which I want to rewrite or revisit. I am not a verse diarist. I don't think of myself changing enormously with circumstance. I don't write very autobiographically in terms of things that happen to me or what I go and do. I chew away at the relationship of my head to the world as I try to understand it, and there's a lot of internalisation going on. And the art changes, the way I want to use artistic methods change. But on the whole, I suppose—although there are vast and very obvious differences—I probably see the rolling collection a bit in the way that Whitman saw *Leaves of Grass*. He saw it as an organism which grew along with his life, and might change and have bits left out and bits added in and bits ... redone in one way or another, or made more sense of as he saw more sense. But I don't think of it as a thing where I move through and reject and lose old things and rejoice at new ones.

JT: You don't rewrite history, in the way that Auden is supposed to have done.

RF: In his own texts? Not a lot, not a lot. Quite a lot of the things I have done within recent years have been lookings-back at myself by way of the texts that I wrote then. And I've seen myself through the way I wrote, and wanted to go back and understand that self better through understanding what those texts are twenty years later. But I don't see my work as a kind of thing like a politician's diary, which I think may be what Auden was thinking of. I don't think I've got that sort of personality.

JT: One thing that's very important in your work, it seems to me, is the influence of place on what you write. It seems you often recreate a place in your work, particularly Birmingham, where you grew up. Now you live out of Birmingham, in the country. I can't imagine two more opposite environments— Birmingham, busy and industrial, completely different to where you live now, which is very quiet, farming country way up in the hills in the middle of England where a car might go by every five minutes.

RF: It's very different. But oddly enough, I don't seem to be able to go to any bit of country without finding traces of mining and industry and people's lives in it. When I was living in Birmingham which I did for forty years, I suppose I was stuck with it like a child out of Wordsworth. For some reason I never really swam in the city as an urban person, although I lived in and around the town a great deal, and was in the pubs and in the jazz clubs and in the educational system of the same place for decades on end. But I was brought up with an implicit belief from my family ... my family who were working people, who seemed to have not long been brought in from the country ... they didn't know anything about the country, they didn't know where they'd come from, but there was a sort of strong moral air that it would be good to get back on to farm land again, and it was something of a pity that they'd had to come in to make a living, that the genes had had to come in two or three generations back, maybe, to be servants or silversmiths or whatever it was. Certainly my father's family, a couple of generations of them, were the sort of working people who got out into the country on bikes and went camping. I was taken for walks in whatever tiny little bit of country there was, and taught flowers and birds' nests, and hills and so forth. It doesn't seem odd to me to live among hills particularly, now. I don't know anything about farming or things like that. But there's an urge to get into that sort of country.

And I suppose the other relation is this, that—what I was trying to say a few minutes ago—that having been brought up in the city—rather as if exiled in it, but exiled from what, I was never told!—I thought of the city as something to question. As I say, I wasn't a real town kid who just withered if shown a cow, you know, the typical town intellectual who says 'Yes, yes, very nice, take me back, take me back before the pubs open.' I wasn't one of those town people, and I just saw it—partly because of a somewhat oblique or withdrawn personality—I just saw it as an agnostic, I had to say 'What is it? What's this great blob? What's this noise, what is all this red brick? Why are people like this?' And in the early poetry, the *City* poetry, I would be trying to more or less put a lever under it and prise it up, historically, and say 'What are these two hundred years that have made this city? That have suddenly made this deposit on the surface of the earth, and has made these activities happen?'

If I live in the country, as I do now, I live in a country which has got a couple of hundred years of petty industrial history, which you can see. And I also live among deposits which are three to four thousand years old. There are Bronze Age tombs on the skyline out of the window. And I think I learn a bit more history, or I learn a bit more intuitive sense of history. So always I'm looking at development and growth and the way people use land, the way people inhabit the surface of the earth. For me it's just a matter of looking at it with a rather longer view. It's odd. I'm living in the middle of what is quite remote country, you can feel remote in it, but I'm told that half the population of England live within fifty or sixty miles in the ring of industrial cities that are all around this green upland. And a lot of my working life consists of going out and giving readings in those cities, or teaching writing workshops in those cities, or playing the piano in the hotels and jazz clubs of those cities. I'm there quite a lot. I sleep in the country.

RF: I'll read a few excerpts from the long poem I wrote four years ago, which is called *A Furnace*. It's built very much on the lines of other modern long poems—it's a collage of various sorts of experience, some of them what I can only call cultural, some of them autobiographical, some of them are a working over of what I think now about things I've written before. And I suppose if it's got a theme, it's an attempt to place my understanding of how the civilisation I was brought up in, which is working class life in a large industrial city which has been invented for people who are not most of the people who live in those cities—an examination of that whole cultural era, that historical era, the two hundred years or so which brought heavy industry, which invented the heavy industrial city, and has—while I've been watching it, while I've been writing about it—allowed it to cease and be dismantled and turned into computer businesses and unemployment programs and leisure parks and things of this sort. I've watched that happen. And I suppose the thing that very much makes the material of the poem is the fact that those cities are huge sudden objects,

94

they are icons, they are ju-jus, they are idols and gods, there are huge physical structures on the surface of the earth which were thrown up.

I was brought up in the shadow of these things, huge black iron constructions turning to half-mile stretches of rust, great monstrosities, things belching smoke and so on and so forth. These were my environment, and I'm very interested in where they came from, and where they've now gone, because they're disappearing as soon as I look at them. You can go to steel towns or coal mining areas and see them razed flat and turned into other things. You can see the good old human race at work making itself comfortable, making itself rich, blotting out what it's doing. That interests me.

And I suppose what I wanted to do in this poem was to say 'How do I know what I know? Who am I? Who is the observer?' It's an attempt—without sitting down to it and writing a five page autobiography—an attempt, by illustrating the way I see, and the way one thing connects with another, to show what sort of an observer I was. And it talks about my education, and the way in which I consider that that education taught me not to see what was in front of my eyes. And anything I have seen, I've only seen by virtue of having been very inattentive or rebellious at school, and looking at what was out of the corner of the picture, what was outside the frame.

[reads from *A Furnace*, Section II, 'The Return']

.... This was a poem where I knew that I'd somehow got to convey I suppose two things, one of which is fairly easy for me after a few decades of practice, which is to say what I've seen, to notate, to report. Because I suppose you get used to describing in terms that people can say 'Yes, I see that. You can draw.' The other thing which is very difficult for me is to somehow enact what I can only call my cast of mind, you know, the angle that the world hits me at, and what it does to me. I take it that this is the most difficult thing that anybody has to do, and maybe some poets can learn to do it quickly and deftly, by how they describe, and I suppose I'm fairly used to being able to get a cast of mind by moving through a bit of material quickly, what you might call an acute state of the cast of your mind. If we're thinking of Frank O'Hara, you pick a little thing like 'Lana Turner Has Collapsed' or 'The Day Lady Died', where so much comes through in a little diagonal passage of that man's mind, through a newspaper event or through a public event.

What I find is difficult is to somehow convey what it's like to be in my head for a week or a month, as various sorts of material—some of which doesn't get conversed about, but is just moods, or is ways of reprocessing experience and joining new experience up to old experience—to somehow find an notation for what that's like. I'm stuck with wanting to do that. So all I could think of to do in this poem was not to pitch against Pound, but to make, in a similar way to all the books of *Paterson*, or whatever you like, an accretive work, where the thing is written in a sequence which is to me musical, but it is at the same time a heap, it's an arrangement, which is not narrative, it's an arrangement in the familiar style of the modern long poem, from any time in the last sixty or seventy years, one of the styles of the modern long poem, the collage. Where you revisit various themes at various times in the course of a thousand or two thousand lines.

If you read it once, and you read it again, they'll start to chime together. And the systems in the poem ... for instance, there's a system to do with identities which is a word that pops up in that sequence a few times, but at one point it's been laid down, and it's chimed on, as if it were an orchestral work, certain instrument sounds, certain bell sounds, and anybody who is patient enough, and is going to give his life up [laughs] to moving through this poem a few times is at least going to be helped by the formal recurrences of a certain bit of vocabulary, or certain icons, you know, like the old woman in black sitting by the wall, there'll be several old women in the poem, there's a system.

When I call it a system, I don't mean a mathematically worked-out system, but there's a reference system like the blood or the lymph, that passes through the poem, which is various ways of treating death. There's an on-going discussion of death, whether the reader likes it or not. I'm talking about death quite a lot, and I'm like this evangelist who's at your elbow, saying 'Talking about death ... we just had this bit about sex and drink or whatever and birth, I was thinking about death while we were doing this, so let's think about death again for a bit, and the burial of the dead.' I go back to it because that's the thing I'm riding through the poem.

So ... I think this is a distinct crunch and difficulty for anybody writing a long poem made of poetry, which is intended to be made of poetry rather than hung on narrative or hung on a lot of anecdote, but which is made chiefly for being in a language which is somewhat freed from anecdote, and is made to move in its own way. If you have a long poem made of poetry, I think we're stuck with having to ask people to float on it and hang around it as they hang around a work of abstract art, or a sizeable symphonic work which they can't tap their foot to all the way through. People do this with music. They will expose themselves to a symphony and see what sticks, see what the character of it is. Later they will understand the themes.

I have to say the poem was not written to be broadcast at long stretches and got in one.

JT: It was written to be read off the page, wasn't it?

RF: It's written to be pored over. I also wanted to write it as something which I could read with pleasure myself, as a sound sequence. I didn't want it to be a cut-up, I didn't want it to be a bag of bits. I did want it to have a certain amount of forward progression, in the sense of the episodes beating along through it. At least that was what I was after.

JT: How has the poem been responded to by people who've read it or reviewed it?

RF: Not badly. I don't think I've encountered reviews which say, oh what the hell, this is a self-indulgent piece of pomposity. What's happened is that the quick reviews tended to say 'This work is a bit more humane than we're used to with Fisher. There are actually some people in it, there's actually a bit of emotion, a bit of political snarling, indignation, anger even. There is supposed to be. It's certainly there in me. Whether it's in the poem ... is not for me to say, but people immediately seem to get a feeling that just possibly, by going on at greater length than I often do, a certain amount of blood and emotion builds up and is secreted.

Lately—they're just coming in to print—three or four sizeable academic articles have been written—Andrew Crozier, Ian Gregson, Peter Barry have written lengthy articles in which they fitted it to what they know of what I've done before. And they see it as I see it, which is as an elucidation, a sort of long gloss and re-enactment of things which I've blundered into, habits I've blundered into, areas of material ... when I say blundered, I'm not criticising myself—I intended to blunder, I wasn't doing anything else—which I blindfolded myself and went for, twenty or thirty years ago. And I was conscious certainly in this of saying 'I'm a bit clearer in the head, and a bit stronger in the hand—how do I now work over the area I found myself in? How do those things fit to what I understand about history, or the plight of peoples?' They've seen that, and pretty-well they all seem to have seen the same thing, and they've named one or two things which apparently I've inadvertently invented, like a thing called 'mimetic scepticism'. Apparently I do have a technique of describing bits of the world with loving care but in such language as to cast enormous doubt on whether there's anything there at all.

And I suppose I do do this. I'm in the business of doing that, I mean, the tradition of Laurence Sterne and again Beckett, saying 'I see this thing, it's doing this, it's doing that, and do I exist to see it at all? Is language stable?' I'm always asking that. But I don't want to play mere language games. This question of what you can say and in what terms you can try to say anything and what you say will do to somebody—these are all up for question, for me. So I suppose I'm an uncomfortable writer in that sense. I don't intend to be otherwise.

JT: I see some history in your writing, and also some regionalism. And I guess this is compared to New York writers or London writers or writers from Melbourne Australia. I was wondering how you see the work you do as part of a tradition that might touch on the work of Geoffrey Hill's *Mercian Hymns* on one side and Bunting's *Briggflatts* on the other.

RF: Geoffrey Hill comes from a place really very near to where I come from. He was born around Bromsgrove which I suppose is twenty miles, thirty miles at the most, from where I come from. He comes from a rather similar social class. Obviously enough, he's got a rather different stake in matters from mine. He's—I think—always more structured and more controlled.

Probably for geographical reasons I found *Mercian Hymns* more to my liking than I think the people I normally run with would expect me to. It is thought of as tending to make a political sound, or an aesthetico-political sound far to the right of what I'm about. And there is this priestly and hieratic quality which some of the people who like what I like would think of as rather tight and bombastic. I was caught by it very much, and the atmospheres of what goes on in *Mercian Hymns*, they rang true for me in all sorts of ways. The idea of there being a history of quite savage energy which is almost recoverable from the body of Middle England, that seems to me worth looking at and worth exploring. I'm probably a lot less interested in kings and hierarchies and great public deeds than he is. But I think there's something there.

And I did indeed once write a poem for him, which was a curious little thing. It's called 'Staffordshire Red' and it arose from an incident where I was driving on a sunless day, so that I couldn't find my bearings from the sun, through a fairly featureless but rather intricate bit of landscape in North Staffordshire, and I found myself, as I felt, 'driving through' a poem by Geoffrey Hill. And it's where a road goes through a sudden cleft in a sandstone cliff with trees arching above it, and I said 'I'm in a poem by Geoffrey Hill'. And I wrote this poem for him, and sent it to him, and the next time we met he said rather savagely 'What are you doing in my imagination?' So I said 'As a Midlander, I have a perfect right to inhabit that bit of Mercia.'

Again, as a man with, I think, an easier access to a historical sense, he was able to move—as he always has been able to move—into other cultures and into earlier bits of England, of English history, into the Tudor or mediaeval periods, the Plantagenet period and into the Saxon period, more easily than I could. I didn't have much of a sense of history to start with, and I acquired it very gradually. It was a thing I was conscious of not having, just like people know they're tone deaf. I get very interested in acquiring more, now. I drift into the past and try to find my feet there. He probably was at ease there; more at ease than he was in the present, much earlier in life than I was.

JT: What about *Briggflatts*? It appears to me to have some connections with what you were doing with Birmingham, in a way. You're not alike at all, but ...

RF: Mmmm.

JT: Compared to, say, Peter Porter, or ...

RF: Oh yeah ... We would be different sorts of Roman poet, wouldn't we? I suppose Bunting and Porter and I would be listening to classical poetry in different ways, and they will know much more about it than I do, having the languages and all. But I suppose where I would come at all into the same area as Basil Bunting is in that particular thing I've tried to express, the difficulty of showing your cast of mind in an extended form of—how did I put it?—trying to illustrate what it's like to be in your head for a day or a week.

And the way in which *Briggflatts* [is] dealing with its own materials, going back to Eric Bloodaxe, going back to personal memory, having a swipe at London, or Paris, quite freely, as if there was no such thing as sequential time, as if everything was in a dream-time of things which are mythic, and a thing which could be a little adolescent moment, or the ride in the cart, it could have happened in Homeric times, it could have happened, it did happen in the Homeric time of a person's own life—this is a different time from chronological time.

In an autobiographical bit I was writing recently I found myself saying that there was a rather dramatic illness I had when my life was at risk for whatever while, when I was twelve, it was an attack of pneumonia which took me away from the world for a while, and in that little bit of pre-adolescence, I found I was living as a convalescent in the place to which I go now to be able to write. And what I found myself saying was that in that place—I'm not twelve again, but it's a place where I don't have to bother to grow old. It's a timeless place. And I can take modern and really awfully grown-up experiences into that place, and the boy of twelve accepts them.

And I think what Basil did classically in *Briggflatts* is to establish a timeless time. You're conscious of time passing, you're conscious of the faculty of memory, and the faculty of search in memory, and the bringing of life from the past. I suppose that, yes, I would want to do that. I want to be free to go from Achilles, as I understand Achilles, who is a person in the book, to my great-great-great uncle William Fisher, who is a figure in a census return which I happen to have read on a microfiche. It's Homeric for me. As are certain moments from my own life.

Bunting's obsession was his aesthetic, his physical obsessions are different from mine, and he's not a man for acres and acres of brick and rust and greasy canals. But it's very clear to anybody who reads Briggflatts and hears the music what the sensory world of Bunting's mind was. You have it there.

JT: I don't think this is a very important point, but I should mention it. It seems to me from the perspective of Australia that your work is more 'American' than 'English' English. Have you run into that problem in England as an English poet? That people have said 'Well he's not really English at all, he's more American than English, therefore we don't like him, or we don't understand what he's trying to do.'

RF: I've been puzzled over. You know there are various little labels that get put on you, and these get parroted from year to year without being updated. There's one which still gets said, which is that 'Roy Fisher is far better known in America than he is in Britain'. I rather wish that this were so, but it hasn't been true since about 1960 when I was slightly known in America and not known at all in Britain.

In fact almost all my currency, so far as I know, is in Britain, and it occurs through two things. One is that I have written to some extent about city life and the actual physical being of cities. And since an enormous number of people have been exposed to that, even though they may not see things the way I see it, they're quite glad to read something which deals with that material fact. And I've got another constituency, which is among young poets, or younger poets and maybe some artists who are quite at ease with the kind of aesthetic I have, or the kind of interest in form that I have. I don't think that I've had much currency in the United States since the United States became fairly self-sufficient in its own poetry, and had plenty of American things to go looking at.

I've never been accused of making 'the mid-Atlantic noise'. There are good poets like Lee Harwood who are accused of making 'the mid-Atlantic noise', and if you do that, in this hard little island, you forfeit your passport. Nobody needs listen to you. And people like Lee, who can move very freely from the American/French-or-Continental world that the New York writers of the sixties had, and is clearly an English writer, I think probably loses a constituency through being so free.

I've obviously got such clearly English problems—I don't mean problems of character, I mean problems of substance, that I was stuck to the place I came from and the questions it gives rise to, for half a century pretty well, and don't write a lot of tourist poetry either, and don't write poems about poetry cliques and parties.

The fact that I did that makes it clear that I'm not an émigré, I don't suddenly start writing tourist poems about American style, about American lifestyle. At the same time I felt free to use American methods because I haven't noticed that there are English methods ready to hand. I could find English methods from English eccentrics, English surrealists for instance, or English nutters— they might as well be painters, I've used bits out of Francis Bacon in my time.

… I tend to want to feel quite internationalist about this, in that I suppose so far as I'm conscious of latching on to methods I've seen used in any literatures in particular, on the whole the methods I want to use I've not seen used with determination, or professionalism if you like, much, in England. We had all sorts of experimenters popping up and popping down; on the whole I tend to think of them as 'gentleman amateurs', or short-fuse people, who'll make a sudden streak, and do one thing, but don't have too much theoretical sense. Whereas it doesn't seem to me, as it never seemed to me, at all unnatural to say 'What had Mallarmé to say on a certain matter? What was Aleksandr Blok doing, where does this relate to Valéry?' And as I talk, I talk off the top about Beckett or Kafka. If I think of the Americans, it's merely the faculty of the Americans, which they showed early in the century, for being open, such of them as were open to anything, of being open to modernism in the first twenty years of the century.

The Armory Show, Williams, Stieglitz, all that lot. They would have a go. They hadn't got the English defences against it. The English defences were canny and preposterous, and are still up. And half the time I take methods which I don't think of as being particularly contemporary in any sense. I will scrabble around in methods that were pushed out anytime between Baudelaire, certainly Mallarmé, and Dada, which still seem to me to be available in kit form if I want to use them, pragmatically, for materials I've got.

And, yes, I suppose the American label does come from the fact that in my own language—I'm no linguist, I can cope with French, and know what happens in German; apart from that I'm in translation—if I want my Russians I have to have them in translation, the Germans too, really; Italians—but yes, the general openness to Modernism, and an attitude to literature which treats it as a matter of composition in the way that painters are used to thinking, musicians are used to thinking—the English language access to that has obviously been more in American writers than in native English writers.

THEY ARE ALL GONE INTO THE WORLD:

Roy Fisher in conversation with Peter Robinson

PR: 'If I didn't dislike / mentioning works of art', the poem 'If I Didn't' from 1975 begins; four years later, the first part of 'The Open Poem and the Closed Poem' mentions four works of art by you. Nobody's suggesting that you can't, like Whitman, contradict yourself, and without contraries there would be no progression; still, striking signs of growth and change begin to show around the beginning of the 1980s, no more directly than in 'The Lesson in Composition' of 1982 with its plain speaking close: 'I'm old enough to want to be prosaic; / I shall have my way'. What do you think was going on with the poetry in those years?

RF: What was going on was the gradual application of hindsight to whatever it was I'd blundered my way into twenty years before. That application generated occasional outcrops of summary, labelling, explicitness. In the poems I mention works of art just as I'd mention anything else. They're not a special category, removed by their mystique. The little flurry at the beginning of 'If I Didn't' simply registers a habitual discomfort with the need to cross a threshold from experience to some sort of transmissible object. In terms of what the poem actually does, it's redundant: my work begins with 'the parapet has already started...' But I wanted to leave that preliminary fidget there for a context. Poems are works of art and mention themselves anyway: that's an element to be taken account of and managed in the process of composition. Where the element's doubled by the additional presence of art as an ostensible subject the handling can run into difficulties—typically, for me, a frictionless slither some writers might find exhilarating: not me. I'm reminded that when we studied Browning at school there'd be long, earnest, experience-free discussions of the fairly simple antinomies in poems like 'Andrea del Sarto' and 'Fra Lippo Lippi'. Apart from occasionally recalling with envy the account of Lippi's untrammelled representationalism, I've hardly thought of those poems in fifty years, but the shallow grooves of those lessons may have continued to dictate some of my tracks ever since. A seamless aestheticism would come quite easily to me, technically, but I shy away from it. I've a hunch, which doesn't have to be right, that I'm better occupied sitting on the edge repeatedly looking awkward than smoothly disporting myself at large out on the oily swell. From time to time I'm impelled to small sceptical perambulations—which I don't, incidentally, see as acts of commitment to postmodernism: there's still such a thing as honest doubt. (I say that in case Davie didn't). It's rather like setting myself the task of punching my way out of a paper bag. Quite easy but rewardingly noisy. I never get into the plastic ones.

PR: 'The Open Poem and the Closed Poem' : you sound like you're taking a sardonic look at poetry-critical stereotyping with that title?

RF: The poem's a pair of caricatures on the same theme. The first is straight, and hence virtually incoherent, reportage of how things were for me in 1979— out of control—with my works of art floating among the other detritus just as if they were mislaid lecture notes or missed engagements, things I was incapable of caring for. The second is the sort of text which might occur in *The Cut Pages* or the remoter stretches of *The Ship's Orchestra*. It's wholly fictive, not susceptible to paraphrase, apparently hermetic in that there's no way it can be 'entered' with the aid of biographical tools; it's linguistically capricious: it's as compact and pocketable as the other is dishevelled. A little work of art, of course, as it well knows.

PR: In the first part you end by wanting 'to have things clear, the circumstances / answerable for a start, so that it's plain who's talking'. The near absence of indirection is perhaps what startles and upsets those devoted to your more oblique methods?

RF: It's worth remembering that the 'prosaic' voice heard barking in 'The Lesson in Composition' is many years younger than I am. There's a tone of Caspar Hauser about it. The poetic 'persona' I had through the 1950s was a strange entity which I carefully preserved in an unstable state, ready for whatever mutation imaginary forces outside my knowledge might impose on it. Deriving its idea of authority from my copious dreams rather than my actual circumstances, it lived in the expectation of experiencing transforming revelations and encounters. Although I never destroyed it (look at the date on the 'Introit' to *A Furnace*) it was quite incapable of taking part in decent writing, for its posturing wrecked poem after poem, and it had to be put to silence. The 'persona' which then came through was more often an absence; when it started speaking out occasionally it could be diffident, as in 'Wonders of Obligation', or brusque, not too particular about choosing its words.
 So. If there's development in the period you singled out, it may be a matter of necessary tidying up rather than breaking ground.

PR: Recalling the shortage of work I tended to encounter when asking you for poems to print in little magazines, it has crossed my mind that 'Wonders of Obligation' refers to your surprise at what being obliged to write had somehow produced. How do you take the poem's title regarding its self-granted permissions to varieties of subject and address? You really didn't see it as a break-through at the time?

RF: The title 'Wonders &c' means what you suggest. It arrived by way of the curious Roman Catholic term 'holidays of obligation' as I considered a field of paradox which it took the poem to lay out. It's a refinement of what I said before about my early assumption of undefined external authorities for the imagination, something documented, with various quasi-theological slants, across the whole canon of Romanticism, usually with the corollary that the authority can manifest itself in any phenomenon, however apparently inconsequential.

PR: A refinement?

RF: Whereas in the 1950s I seemed to have no choice but to approach the world's revelations via a persona I can only call, in the kindliest way, stupid, here I was interested in remaining sharply conscious throughout. The idea of revelation is, of course, a projection of the condition of the perceiving self—it's not that I believe there to be a troupe of Beings behind a curtain, poking meaningful things through—and by this time I wanted to exercise a perception that felt itself to be in better shape: maybe a little less self-enclosed, for one thing, a little more companionable. What I mean by 'obligation' is that we're obliged by our senses, insofar as they're not subjected by cultures to various quaint patterns of occlusion, to pay attention to the entire array, in order to find what's safe and what's not, and so forth. I've been strongly aware of this since as far back as I can remember, which is a long way. I was a child who made a detailed perceptual vocabulary from the physical properties of things, mostly at floor level, indoors and out (it's still chaotically active within reach, hardly bedded down at all, never discredited) while being alienated from anything that came mediated through pronouncements, even when they imposed on me and controlled my life.

PR: There's the passage about 'the poor of Birmingham', the mass graves dug for those killed in bombing raids, and the fear of being treated like a pauper among poor city people like my father's mother—lines Jon Silkin responded to in his last book *The Life of Metrical and Free Verse in Twentieth-Century Poetry*, though he calls the poem as a whole 'evasive, slippery, characteristically deliquescent'.

RF: As for the form, I saw it as my job to lay my particular set of wonders out on a stall, uniformly priced so far as I could force that appearance upon them, contrary to the habits of the culture. Which habits I wasn't attacking; simply sidestepping. Like most writers I've reason to know the futility of trying to dictate the details of different readers' responses to the same text, and here I knew that if the poem acquired any readers they'd be laying their several minds across it like sensitised sheets of paper, and would print their own patterns of emphases, all different, according to what they brought. I wanted to avoid pre-dramatising the materials: for me that wouldn't be art, it would be hokum.

PR: Have you ever used dice-throwing or paper out of a hat techniques to produce chance organisations of material?

RF: I'm familiar with aleatoric techniques in all the arts, but, while not disapproving, have to live with a fading of my appetite for the game after only a short journey along that road. I'm not much inclined to appear as a character in a piece of this sort, but I like to be present as the conductor, exercising a certain flair, of a linear progression—and that's most certainly a game, for I'm well aware that the mind's operations aren't linear. It's like music, where the experience starts from zero information and acquires patterns from the information that's fed on a controlled time-line.

PR: Andrew Crozier has described 'Wonders of Obligation' as a 'celebration of the multiplicity of the particular' and a 'rite de passage' that makes possible the 'imaginative self-definition' in *A Furnace*. But perhaps Crozier's 'celebration of multiplicity' genially generalises the sections about the boys' silliness in the school jakes, the 'Wigan pisspot' (from Orwell, I imagine), or your classmates in 'the intake of '35'?

RF: From where I was when letting the various materials into the poem I didn't see the more political or social items—those with class-system markers on them—as being of a different order: the social class was my own, and though it no longer exists I haven't knowingly signed up to any other. It goes without saying that certain materials in any text are more volatile than others: it depends where the readers' hungers and attention-triggers lie. War gets regarded as automatically 'serious', but in the passage about the mass graves the presence of the War marker is incidental to the trickier business of drawing the sensation of living in a governed city.

At the end of the poem you can indeed see me handing round the pisspots, intent on imposing pattern. The Wigan one was brought to mind by the thought that some time around that day—17 June 1935—when I was brought inescapably face to face with 'the others' for the first time, my mother's apron strings having been short and strong, Orwell in Wigan was suffering the shock of meeting the charged chamber-pot as it was borne down the stairs of his lodgings. And that took me to that rhapsodic passage in Coleridge (*Notebooks* I think—can't now trace it) about sunlight on urine.

'Slithering' eh? For two almost exact contemporaries who often collaborated, Jon and I were about as different in temperament as could be. If my way's centrifugal and pluralistic his was centripetal and concentrated. When I wrote 'Matrix' he asked for it, and I sent it with the suggestion that he might like to publish a few of its sections. He was, however, keen to publish it entire, while confessing himself to be in the unusual position of wishing to endorse a work whose mode of articulation he couldn't get into focus. I felt obliged to assure him he wasn't accepting a suspect package.

PR: Silkin cites lines from 'Wonders' that probably struck a chord with his own wartime and gravedigger materials, but not the flying leap by which readers find themselves transported into the cockpit of a Dornier or Heinkel bomber over Birmingham: 'down in the terraces between the targets, / between the wagon works / and the moonlight on the canal'.

RF: I'm interested to see you pick up the air raid in 'Wonders' as a whole picture, not just a cry of victims. Anybody who experienced those heavy night raids will probably remember how ponderous and slow they could be. Before the explosions and the gunfire the sound was that of a number of laden lorries or buses a mile or so off—straight up—and it wasn't difficult to imagine men like lorry-drivers shoving them along.

PR: I see your point about the poem's materials not being stacked and presented with too many hierarchical, perspectival, or tendency relevance markers attached, though would guess you can't get round (and needn't want to) such things as nature/culture distinctions that are embedded in the grammar of the language...

RF: No indeed, as regards 'nature' and 'culture', I wasn't concerned to flatten the language's naturally-acquired contours completely; merely to deflate excrescences of drama I didn't want.

PR: That 'stupid' persona is what gets you signed up with the much-reiterated 'making strange' business, I imagine, a persona that (in 'As He Came Near Death', for instance) has to pretend to know nothing about hospitals and cemeteries. There is a freshness in finding that the later work's characteristic registerings of perception and experience don't have to go with a 'born yesterday' relation to life.

RF: Was it Davie who brought that 'making strange' business in? I've never traced it back to its source, but I know some people—maybe you—have, for I've seen it set out. At any rate, the 'naïf' technique of 'As He Came...' is just that—a technique, lightly taken on in a sort of proto-Martian way so as to invite a slight rearrangement of the reader's possibly settled perceptions by taking a thin slice of the descriptive menu. I didn't get a preview from the Martians: it's a very old device.

PR: Well, no; 'As He Came...' can't possibly have been prompted by one of Raine's sorties into the oddity of contemporary domestic appliances and fixtures. If anything, he might have been prompted by your *Interiors* poems and related work from over a decade before the Martians landed. As you say, it's a hoary old device, and Raine too may have got it at source.

RF: Some such technique is virtually obligatory in musical variation, in whatever idiom. The stated melody has to be ritually thrown off balance, subtly and gradually or by a sudden onset, in order to activate it to move to a new equilibrium by way of the creation of previously unknown material.
 In language, a less abstract medium and vastly more viscous, merely to divert a string of syntactically secure conversational language to a path only a little to one side of its expected register will inevitably make for a first level of strangeness, even without advancing into the disruption and rearranging of

small packets of linguistic energy.

All this, however, is distinct from the 'stupid' persona of my twenties, hardly visible in any of the published work. The character I assumed when entering on a poem then wasn't innocent, or even conscious, in a stylistic sense: the model was that of a submissive candidate for initiation into a mystery religion, drugged, hallucinated, hungry for oracular news. Honestly. I don't know now where it came from, but I know where it went.

In the 1950s hardly any of the poems where I—wearing my persona—chose a subject and approached it directly turned out to be publishable, much though I admired them myself. Usually (list on application when I've made it) I'd work from some random starter or other and see what it set off, getting out of my own self-conscious way. 'Lesson in Composition' again refers.

PR: You have a passage in *A Furnace* where binary distinctions get a stern telling off as the means for subjugation in 'the devil his grammar school, / wherein the brain / submits to be / cloven'. That passage is part of a section that ends 'the life of the dead'. What's that? You're having to run hard against the habits of ordinary usage to get out of the devil's grammar school there, aren't you?

RF: I don't have a lecture to deliver on this. It's just a swipe at one of those obligatory blessings—the body, parents and so on—that plague us so. One reason for the sheer length of *A Furnace* was my wish to avoid repeatedly setting out my terms, as in a free-standing shortish poem. I wanted to have something rolling wherein I could dive into a topic without announcing it and then go on, hoping readers who were willing to ride the poem might have picked up my tone and be able to follow it into odd corners.

This brings me back to an earlier comment about my pragmatic interest in the straightforwardly linear. It puts me into the situation of having to attempt the classical thing—looking for a way of saying something once which any reasonable person would say at least twice, from different directions so as to get a decent stereo image. For me it leads, since I don't want to digress, into the use of shorthands—paradox and metaphor. I think I probably use paradox a good deal. I don't like elaborating my own metaphors or creating setups with them since I'm working in a language by now largely made up of composted metaphors and sunken puns; I don't like to bring on heavy play that might rupture the delicate web of tendrils. It's all right in conversation, as here.

PR: And 'the life of the dead'...

RF: I was fishing to see what an inchoate scrap of metaphysic might turn up. For no reason I could predict, the succeeding passage told itself in what still seems (I'm somewhat external to it) to want to add itself to the world in its own terms. A familiar excuse for inability to paraphrase.

PR: You've raised a couple of conceptual issues I'd be interested in a further response to: one is the aleatory; the other the notion that some defamiliarising is a familiar feature of poetic language. Anyone presenting a bundle of words for making public (even if the words have been randomly brought together with a dice or top hat or the *I Ching*, and the making public is as minimal as we know it can be in this game) anyone doing this is performing at least three or four intentional acts, acts which invite interpretation—often of a paradoxically stipulatory kind. Isn't the overriding experience of reading, even some such extremely recalcitrant aleatory text, one of familiarity? As my first wife once put it when asked to comment on the nth version of some piece I was struggling with: 'I've seen all these words before, but never in quite this order!' Then there's the fact that people who are seriously interested in a poem and a poet (to echo 'Sets') will also take the thing or things at fairly regular intervals. For me, the pleasure of 'The Cut Pages' is partly one of an old friend. I know how it goes on, absolutely in the same old way.

RF: Your observation about the way readers revisiting a text, even one designed to have no guidance as to its use, will tend to fix their own readings—to 'see' patterns in a display which at first suggests none—is certainly true to my experience, just as it's familiar to perceptual psychologists. The matter's sophisticated when we're dealing as we are in the arts with affectively and referentially complex particles. I've a simple example on this desk: a notebook into which I've put, over eighteen years now, scraps of language—names, overheard phrases, inventions, fragments popping into recall from childhood reading—which caught my fancy in a particular way, dropping them into the pages randomly through the whole book so as to deprive them of a time-scale. I knew from the first that they would inevitably form what I'd see as relationships with their neighbours; and so they did. When I now insert a fresh item into a space on an occupied page the old inhabitants show various forms of excitation; if I lift one out for use elsewhere it registers disorientation. And to read the book from Page One is to submit myself to a story I didn't devise. And so on.

The notion of the automatic estrangement of language by virtue of its being in a poem is an assumption I've never tested. I'm thinking of the way a poem, to a more or less marked degree, shows itself to be a closed language-system. It may resemble other such systems as much as unexamined fingerprints do, but the dynamic of its field has to be unique. A relentlessly populist technique like Larkin's ('Reader, you see as I see: there's no other way. Therefore you can't but think as I do...') goes to some lengths to erase the signs of separateness. A signal example of another direction would be Wallace Stevens, where the robust conventional syntax combines with his disingenuous gumshoe metrics to march lexis—often in repetitiously re-vamped systems—into territory it, and its familiar users, could never have imagined.

That said, it's immediately apparent that a writer's linguistic disposition will usually leak from poem to poem, as Stevens's specialised vocabulary does.

I'm not much of a single poem man, either as reader or writer. As a reader I'm looking for the consistent features across a poet's language. As a writer I know that my individual poems are usually either concerned with the winkling out and working up of some small suspected germ of a notion or are single sweeps of the net through profuse material.

PR: Do you think of 'The Cut Pages' as a text which sets out to disrupt, undercut, undermine, and all that?

RF: I've certainly never set out to demonstrate the possibilities of such manipulations and am hence much less 'experimental' than I'm sometimes said to be. To demonstrate, to claim—that sounds to me a bit social, a bit interventionist. A few buffooneries apart, all my writing comes from my introversion. Inevitably, it's at odds with my exhibitionism, but that's a condition shared by many. My 'experiments' are pragmatic, done to show me how far my range can go. They never advance as far as theory or prescription: the doors of the School of Combined Honours in Moral Theology and Fashion Studies are closed to me. 'The Cut Pages' for instance, as anti-authorial a piece as I've done, will be more to the taste of some readers for that reason. It's like that, though, for no firmly theoretical reason but because I had a strong operational need at that time and in those pages to blank out signs of authorial presence.

PR: Could 'The life of the dead' section of *A Furnace* be at least flirting with the possibility that a poem will console its readers? Doesn't the passage offer resources for dealing with bereavement that are not available in quite this form elsewhere?

RF: There's a small estrangement in the phrase. A good deal of what I'm on about is the lives of the dead, their lost histories. Making it singular makes it, by intention, a more abstract and extensive term which has to take its chance. *A Furnace* is in large part a piece of frustrated ancestor-worship, a running of a familiar type of tribal model over whatever recent history shows up on the ground. Politics. You may be interested, or shocked, to learn that the straight autobiographical piece 'They Come Home' from *Birmingham River*—about my wife Joyce's parents who had died within a fortnight of each other in 1980— sat for a while before *A Furnace* was published in its 'Core' section. The piece beginning 'That sky-trails may merge...' was originally two, the second beginning 'We're carving the double spiral...' 'To bring back the parents...' formed a lengthy spacer. I've not tried the effect of replacing it.

As for whether my attempt to find some form of community with the dead has the power to comfort or enlighten anyone else: well, I can't count on it. It certainly made sense for me to be keeping company with the subject in a stark and placid frame of mind when I was writing.

PR: I'm not shocked, or surprised for that matter, to hear that the marvellous 'They Come Home' is an out-take from *A Furnace*. But let me link it up with another poem in *Birmingham River*: 'Going'. In that poem's blank ending 'And they're gone, that's all' you seem to be repudiating or denying what you've called 'my attempt to find some form of community with the dead' in the long poem, and it seems to run imaginatively counter to the exhortation in 'They Come Home' that we should 'by no means separate the dead / from anything'. A critic might be tempted to venture that there's a metaphysical and an empiricist 'Roy Fisher' battling it out here. As the empirical Roy Fisher, do you see 'Going' as in conflict with, say, 'The Return' section of *A Furnace*, with 'They Come Home', or the encounter with the hanged boy in 'The Dow Low Drop'?

RF: I'm agreeable to being many-mouthed or many-headed, but I don't relish being cloven, since that would imply a rejection from Position B of what Position A had to say. 'Going' is a short yelp—prompted by events—from somewhere further round the same mountain. The more spread treatments in *A Furnace* come from a disposition to diffuse death through my territory, whereas in 'Going', Death, the Sniper, was taking all the initiatives. (A couple of widows had said to me 'then John/David fell at my feet as if shot'). I've a hunch that had 'Going' turned up five or six years earlier I might have found a way of fitting it into *A Furnace* somewhere, as a sharp-edged fragment in the general flow. It wouldn't have occurred to me that it was in contention with anything else I said.

I agree that it's no shame for poets to be puzzling together about death and the way it lives with us. Proper work. At the same time I have to watch myself: I said recently to somebody that my long file of cemetery pieces has less to do with my limited interest in dissolution than my liking for shooting static targets, a tombstone being less able to wriggle or argue than its occupant when alive.

PR: In need of a title, I once stole a one-line poem of W. S. Graham's, 'Feeding the dead is necessary', which catches for me some of what poets are about in their imaginary graveyards. Are you a reader of his work at all?

RF: Sidney Graham. One of my neglects—even to the extent of having failed to acquire any of his work. In the late 1940s I was reading him with interest as an Apocalyptic (I was one of the bedraggled band of fans who couldn't see why all that was so ridiculed) and kept an eye as far as *The Nightfishing*. When I realised later that he'd survived, developed and remained productive I gave myself a memo to catch up on him, but have still not done so. With his point about the feeding of the dead I'm in complete agreement.

PR: We probably have to feed them because they're feeding us: you have that piece 'News for the Ear' about 'the poet Bunting' who, 'bored with the talk / of the state of literature that year', sinks away 'to his preferred parish /

among old names, long reckonings'. There the dead are a ballast against the familiar storm and stress of ephemera. And in 'The Ticket-of-Leave Man' Bunting is one of the dead who come back in dreams and is treated with over-familiarity by someone. A Furnace has been likened by John Matthias to Yeats's reading of Pound's 'The Return', to a Vorticist force field of energies, and to Constructivism. What John doesn't do is relate the Yeats idea to your sceptical treatment of him as model in the 'Five Morning Poems from a Picture by Manet', or your equally sceptical 'in memoriam' poem for Wyndham Lewis. Those seem early essays in shooting static targets: are they?

RF: The 'Five Morning Poems' sequence is hard for me to make contact with after so long, and I don't think I ever thought of Yeats while writing it. It's not an intentional parody, or even homage. But I know that at that time I will have envied Yeats his armour plate—something I felt the need of for a while as companion for my timidity. In the preceding year or two I'd started to hit readable form, encouraged by the examples of Williams, Olson and Creeley and, with the addition of direct response and guidance, of Turnbull, Corman and Eigner. Where those people were leading me was into an antinomian territory where there was neither external authority nor cover. From the first, I profited: the second I couldn't take. It was a period when my disposition had no cause to be sunny; also, as an habitual mimic, I could tell I needed to avoid facile American mannerisms, which Black Mountain had in plenty. Without recognising that that was what I was doing I retreated from my position of a little advantage, writing things which in theme and form showed a sardonic fatalism, of interest, as it turned out, only to myself, and that only briefly.
        So. I didn't have Yeats in my sights. Lewis, yes, though he wasn't a static target for me, even though newly dead. That remarkable energy might still kick. All I had in mind was to evoke him and his contradictions without analysis but with the ironic use of images from his own paintings and from Guernica.

PR: Has anyone raised the possibility with you that the chief model for A Furnace is Bunting's Briggflatts? Both poems have a journey out and a return, plus a cyclical movement; both are evidently shaped by analogy with musical composition, and both contain mixtures of deep history and personal biography. Did you have Bunting's poem in mind as you were working on the poem?

RF: With the honourable exception of Robert Sheppard in his TLS review, I don't believe anybody has connected A Furnace to Briggflatts, but the link is there. On one level it's a personal one. I was a friend and supporter of Basil during the last twenty years of his life and had a fair idea of his way of working. My first meeting with him was at a private reading of a late draft of Briggflatts. And, quite simply, he was the only poet I've ever known personally who was capable of undertaking a work on that scale and bringing it off. The degree of formal coherence he achieved was in itself a guidance, for you only have to start running the tally of the century's attempts to see how that factor was surrendered or abandoned, for one reason or another—often because of the tendency of a magnum opus to keep treacherously close step with the author's life: *The Waste Land*—filleted and collapsed; *The Bridge*—hysterically overpitched; *The Cantos* and *Maximus* left to run themselves into the sand or expanding cosmic space, respectively, and *Paterson* likewise left with nowhere to go.

PR: Ah, the Nabokovian interview style at last! Time for some football-kicking criticism, and about time too! I have the Yeats idea from a suggestion of yours, though: in the interview with Erwin and Rasula, you say: '"Fiction of understanding worst of all": in that poem, in fact, I talk about ordinary people who die and their death is given ceremony on an almost Yeatsian level'. This doesn't mean you needed to have Yeats in mind at the time, but you did call him up on one later occasion. But let's stick with Bunting for a while. With his 'old names, long reckonings', his interest in the finest minutiae of technique, and, as you say, his formal coherence, he seems a figure like Schoenberg in music: an experimenter steeped in centuries of tradition. His sense of scale is acute too. *Briggflatts* runs to 20 pages in the *Complete Poems*; *A Furnace* covers 37 in your *New and Selected*. These count as long works in the era of pieces that rarely 'turn the page', but they are not literally interminable poems, like some of those you list above. Did the 'double spiral' structure come early in composing the poem, or was it imposed on the material late? Did the formal device help establish your sense of a suitable scale, or keep the thing from spiralling off into the ether?

RF: OK. My shortlist of large-scale poems should have included *The Anathemata*, where the huge collage is articulated by being hung across a world-system which Jones regarded as stable and eternal. I'm not, of course, regretting the absence of coherence and closure in our age's masterworks, merely saying that *Briggflatts* gives hints which their various natures preclude. And I love the tug of it, the way it hauls you through its relatively brief extent.

It is in fact an extraordinarily compressed work. When I was feeling for a length for *A Furnace*, *Briggflatts* was the one I measured, and I was surprised to find how short it was: it reads and resounds like something much more extensive. And at that point I could see that my own poem would need to be twice as long, since I knew my texture couldn't be so dense unless I was actually to parody Bunting's tight, consonant-stiffened lingo, and also since my method was very different from his. He said the text of *Briggflatts* was the residue of an enormous process of reduction from extensive drafts. My poem, on the other hand, was written almost at its final length, with only a few cuts and re-orderings. I've never been able to draft and redraft much: I have to hold things back from taking verbal form in order not to congeal something that wasn't quite what I intended. In that pre-writing stage they're not non-verbal, certainly not mere pictures: they exist in a mode that contains language but doesn't yet demand that the lever be pulled, selecting language as the sole means of apprehension—and, of course, of transmission.

Although *Briggflatts* has plenty of autobiographical material and a wide range of other reference, it's characterised by pulling-together, matching, juxtaposing and grafting: it's a work of summary rather than exploration. Hence its scale and its contained shape. I had something of a similar task in front of me, so I kept those qualities within view.

PR: So what was the task?

RF: For me, an important element in poetry is the arrangement and presentation of fetishes. I don't use the word in a reductive or aberrant sense, or any implication that the harbouring or nurturing of fetishes is something that makes us less than free. It's my password into the business of primary orientation, the way we learn, as young animals with unsorted language and suspicious senses, to negotiate the places and creatures we find ourselves among, and to decide, if we have any choice, where to lodge ourselves in the culture-packages the others live by. In that world, usually a phase that flourishes then gets slimmed down for action, phenomena of no matter what kind can carry a high potential for focusing and channelling energy. Anathemata, wonders of obligation. This preoccupation accounts for the presence of John Cowper Powys in the dedication of *A Furnace* and, in one form or another, in each of its sections. His almost shapeless novels, which offer hardly any foothold for conventional criteria of literary merit, are held together by networks of just such fetishisms—thin bread and butter, weed-grown ponds, walking-sticks, sodden moss—carried forward into the adult lives of his characters and offering, I think, quite different faces of subjective existence to different readers. All I can say is that when I first read him in my early twenties he spoke to my condition, odd as it was.

So I found him an appropriate Virgil for my task of investigating and sorting the crowded cellar of my own subjectivity, which, with the added element of matching up inchoate inner experiences with externally accessible, recorded, public matters, is what *A Furnace* is about. I had a private vocabulary, barely verbalised but sharply evaluative, of perceptions acquired over many years, none of them susceptible to conversion to anecdote or conversation; the terms in the vocabulary were what I've called fetishes, and from these I wanted to create, by making patterns with them, a sort of grammar—something I needed by then for my own comfort, let alone anybody else's understanding. The fetishes were what I called, in the 1986 preface to *A Furnace*, 'obstinate substances', some of them very ponderous. In around 1958-9, when I returned to Birmingham after a few years in Devon, the entire city functioned in that way, while on a finer scale any occurrence of the word 'street' would produce an over-excitation which made me realise something was afoot.

The spiral came in early, as soon as I started taking stock of the material, letting it come into memory, seeing which elements recurred and clustered and demanded inclusion. I'd asked Bunting, not long after the publication of

Briggflatts, to tell me how he'd organised it: expecting a few minutes' explanation, possibly evasive, I was interested to get an early demonstration of the now-familiar five-peaked diagram. It made sense. For *A Furnace* I wanted a single figure, and the returning spiral was ideal for the circling sense of anti-time I was after. It has no central point; as you go in you pass yourself several times on the way out; when you're out you may as well take the next way back in.

As for forward progression, I'd committed myself to whatever I could manage in the way of a line through, in deference to the enslavement of the English language to a word-order syntax, which I'm never much inclined to try to kick. There's always Latin.

The spiral, like many a formal armature, was there as an aid to composition. I did nothing to make it visible, or necessary, to the reader. What I did was draw a spiral, arrow the converse directions of movement, then take a slice across it through the middle. That gave me three ins alternating with three outs, and a middle which could have a stillness or a dual motion. Plus the 'Introit'. I used this shape as a guide to disposing the material among the sections and to get a shadowy, quasi-narrative mood while writing. When reading the poem now I'm not aware of the armature.

PR: In a lighter vein, is 'that sunken boiler, slowly and implacably surfacing of its own / volition—the finest of my ideas!' for which 'you' get a grant that produces instant writer's block, is it not *A Furnace* prefigured in parody? I'm thinking of the passage where the scuttled German High Seas Fleet bobs up to the surface in Scapa Flow, for instance.

RF: You got it. The Grand Fleet, a typical submerged fetish, came up through 'A Modern Story' as, unusually for me, a simile. In *A Furnace* I get it to show out. The spiral at work: a few years later, freelancing and at liberty to look for an Arts Council Bursary (in those days your publisher had to apply on your behalf) I thought a single book-length poem, something I was shaping up for anyway, was the best thing to offer as a project. So I took the occasion to get my ideas into focus, submitted a forecast-sketch of *A Furnace*, and got the bursary. Such was the pressure of honest imaginative need that I felt obliged to write the thing instead of founding a poetry prize with the money. The boiler became a furnace.

PR: 'This age has a cold blackness of hell / in cities at night...Chicago cradles it.' I'm struck by this moment when a city other than English ones crops up in your work. *A Furnace* is distinctive in allowing into the text evidences from the dreaded 'abroad' of Larkinian ill-repute: I'm thinking of Trier, Barnenez, Paris, and Ampurias as well.

Then in poems from *Birmingham River* there's the gulf of Corinth, Drebkau, and a bus stop in Barcelona. The later work seems to have eased up about what can count as your territory, though I notice in the recent 'Four Songs from the Camel's Coffin' that not leaving the British mainland until aged fifty produced a curious sensation on stepping onto the 'battered tarmac of O'Hare'. Is that how Chicago got into *A Furnace*? But you've spoken elsewhere about the biographical circumstance behind this, and for some 30 years English experience seems to have satisfied the poetry's need for concretion. What forced the wider world into the later work?

RF: The sprinkling of civilisation-sites after about 1980 comes mainly from the fact that from that time I became able actually to get to some of them, and since I'm the sort of animal who needs to sniff the air and get the feel of the streets, I couldn't speak of places I'd not experienced. I've talked elsewhere about the travel-phobia, mostly concealed, which afflicted me for a long while. Its history fits neatly with the work, and the sort of life I've always led, best characterised as the ceaseless compulsive accumulation of all kinds of clutter, mostly amiable but adding up to an unending rain of neglected friendships, unread books, unfiled papers, unvisited ideas: bad housekeeping. My sub-generation, prevented by the war from travelling, found it difficult and expensive to take up, except by the exercise of determination. Given my cluttered habits I could never make space to work up such determination, and my fugitive nature at that time made it easy to convert the circumstances into a full-scale inability to undertake more than short journeys by car or train. It was a sort of peripheral agoraphobia: thoroughly at ease within a twenty-mile radius, I'd expect disintegration of the self and the world anywhere beyond. I can remember as late as 1967 suffering mortal dread throughout a drive from Birmingham to Coventry and back.

I'd no aversion to other places, having, in particular, spent much of my life in an America of the mind, but when offered work abroad I'd invent excuses and believe them. In the meantime I learned my own patch, as I wrote somewhere, the way a cat would, or a fox. Beyond that I had virtually no geographical extension, just as I had, until comparatively recently, little sense of history. The aversion to travel had probably dispersed by 1970, but the relentless acquisition of more and more immediacies which my newly patched-up nerve made possible left me no opportunity for taking advantage. It was ten years before I forced myself to take a flight to Chicago to meet the tarmac at O'Hare. After that I made up for lost time. The naming of foreign parts is probably an acknowledgement, maybe in itself unnecessary, that my earlier confinement to local references had an element of morbid necessity about it. The references come in, I think, only when they chime with what I knew or suspected already: there's some build-up of an understanding of history too.

PR: *City* looks like it has a time-span of approximately 1860 to 1960, whereas *A Furnace* has a smattering of dates: 1902, 1861, 1818; then there's that apparition figure, your Dr. Dee or Donne or Lord Chandos; and much further back patches of prehistory in those ancient sites. Did the intersections of '*Landscape superimposed / upon landscape*' and of history superimposed on history impress

117

themselves simultaneously? Is there a question implied in our exchanges here about the relation between agoraphobia and poetic archaeology? The conversation might also scotch a sense of you as a Black Mountaineer. You couldn't have done a poem called 'From Birmingham Out', I imagine; or does *A Furnace* have such an aspect?

RF: The extensions of time and place developed together, or are maybe the same thing. 'Curi-Osity', as Pound pronounced it. They're not a voyage out from the Birmingham of *City* or an attempt to annex additional territories by imperialist naming; more the casting out of lines to stabilise it. The instability of the earlier 'city' is characterised in *A Furnace* III. Authorities; being mostly a subjective creation, a haunting, it's susceptible to collapse. A question not of form but of the initial imagining.

Black Mountain poetics never got to me as a concern with place. At the time I made contact (about 1956 when the College was already in its diaspora) I still had no idea that my work would come to take on that character. What I did pick up was the sense that that was where the needle was vibrating most strongly at that time (as it would be in New York a few years later—but not for me). There were particularly clear indications in the matter of going directly to what you wanted to address, and of changing tack, without any of the huffing and puffing, canvas-stretching and general warm-up techniques I'd acquired unnecessarily. Creeley was an education in small-scale deftness, and even Olson, leaving out the maps and charts, had plenty to show in the way of calling material in from wherever he chose, and slanting it likewise.

PR: You mentioned earlier that 'any occurrence of the word "street" would produce an over-excitation which made me realise something was afoot'. Can you talk a bit about those 'fetishes' you refer to in relation to a poet's obsession with particular words? There was a phase when you seemed compulsively drawn to the word 'nondescript', for instance. Have you ever found yourself editing out signature reiterations of such words?

RF: The 'fetishes' which accumulated over the years to the point where they seemed to need me to articulate them, insofar as I could, in *A Furnace*, were mostly sensory, on a long scale from a nuance of scent or fading light to monstrous architecture and skyscapes. Some of them had been with me a long time. I remember talking about the problem in the mid-1960s with Simon Cutts, a strong-minded poet who was at that time concentrating his force by limiting himself to a light, pinkish boulevardier aesthetic somewhere in Satie territory. I explained how I was hankering after a technique for handling rich and dense materials. 'Oh. That's just greedy,' he said. Which didn't relieve me of my difficulty.

Obviously there are, probably for all writers, obsessive and nearly-inexpressible perceptions which are much less substantial, and it's those which seep into one's grammar, rhythms and entire rhetorical system. Signatures. La patte. I don't spend enough time reading my own work to have analysed my own mannerisms, though I have a rough sense of when my vocabulary's starting to harp on itself to the point where it leaves the general lexical field and constitutes a specialised micro-language. 'Nondescript' is indeed just such a low-level conceptual fetish, a thought-counter which I use much as Sartre might have done. But I wouldn't want to elevate and limit it to the status of the sort of technical term you might find in a philosophical system, or a pseudo-system like Stevens's. If I've done so with an abstraction inadvertently it's a sign I should read myself more. I edit descriptive language and repeated themes more carefully. If there are repetitions there it's because they've nagged.

PR: One or two of the reviewers who welcomed *The Dow Low Drop: New and Selected Poems* mentioned that what is needed, or might come next, is a proper *Collected Poems*. You mentioned to me in our 1977 recorded conversation that there was a notional manuscript called *Underwritings, Overwritings* of early material in existence. Besides retrospective publishing possibilities, I suspect that there must also be a growing sheaf of uncollected recent poems as well. Have you any plans afoot to organise the retrospect, or add another to your published books?

RF: I've never developed much of a feel for the process of publication; virtually all the ideas about bringing my work out have come from other people. As a rule my work has taken me by surprise, so I never formed a policy about what should happen to it beyond the first publication, usually in a magazine or pamphlet. The writings have turned out to be more extensive and varied than I could have expected, and my ad hoc publishing habits have proved unequal to the job, with the result that it's not possible to see how a Complete Works can come about—for some while at least.

I've not thought of such a *Collected* as being a project for me to undertake myself, or have much part in. The temptation to rewrite history's there for an author. Writers suppress pieces which irritate or embarrass them but have interest for some readers, who can be baffled to see the author changing his self-portrait. There are plenty of examples. And I've never felt comfortable about periodic collections of miscellaneous pieces, where disparate styles or genres can make the book seem to be contradicting itself.

Not that I'm at all repentant about writing in different manners. For me, styles and genres exist in a continuum, from a level where you can pick language off the top or off the wall and throw it about conversationally, down through degrees of formality to radically disruptive or disjunctive explorations. I don't see any division. To call up Bunting again: his excellence is readily apparent because of his elaboration of a fairly restricted register, somewhere between those extremes. He didn't play radical language-games, but neither was he ever casually colloquial: his familiar conversation was deliberate, and his anecdotes sculptural.

Only a handful of poems completed since *The Dow Low Drop*, so no collection in prospect in any case. I'm most at home with short-run, short-life pamphlets, which can look like single messages. I've at least three promised out, none of them begun yet. I need to have some sort of sense of freedom, real or imagined, in order to write: at present that's hard to come by.

The list of previously-collected work not now in print and/or with the copyrights in my possession includes 'The Cut Pages', the sequences 'Six Deliberate Acts', 'Five Morning Poems', 'Matrix', 'Glenthorne Poems' and 'Handsworth Liberties', plus fifty or sixty single poems and prose pieces. In addition there are over forty published but (for various reasons) uncollected poems which might need looking at. That lot might make a book on its own, should anyone feel like doing it. The alternative could well be to post it on the Internet, as a sort of Cabinet of Curiosities. It would at least make it available, and be quite consistent with my lifelong neglect of the future.

PR: Your continuum of styles must have something to do with the ways you have been taken up, championed, received. A scan of the poetic horizon shows your work being acknowledged by Ian McMillan, a poet close to stand-up comedy, and warmly introduced at a conference on advanced poetics by Peter Riley. We've already touched on what Silkin found to admire. There are aspects of your work that hold the attention of Marjorie Perloff, Crozier, or Andrew Duncan, and selected others that have been appreciated by D. J. Enright and Davie. Then there is Jeremy Hooker's support for a late but flourishing romantic landscape artist, while Matthias appears to combine that strand with a view of you sustaining early modernist strategies. Notwithstanding your own neglect of the future, it's tempting to see your work as sponsoring poetry's future on a host of apparently conflicting fronts. What do you make of all this?

RF: Your question arrived at the same time as an advance copy of Sean O'Brien's *The Deregulated Muse* in which I'm characterised as 'the modernist (and postmodernist) the non-modernists enjoy and to some extent understand'. I haven't much to say about it except to swear that all these appreciations are unsolicited.

Neither are they, so far as I can see, any more contradictory than the work itself is. And you'll have seen that I resist that diagnosis. At this stage I've a hankering for finding consistency in what I've done, which is why I nowadays find myself willing to add text to texts in the form of comments like these, anthropomorphic though they may appear. The consistency I'm after includes some account of the failures—of intelligence, technique or nerve, or things I'm not myself aware of—on the assumption that the way they lie in the overall shape may be of interest to somebody.

The authors of the range of comments you list are mostly people who know a thing or two, and who know their own ground well enough to understand that I, in turn, know mine. And maybe, in their disparate natures, they get a lift from seeing that quality in another writer, regardless of what my particular interest may be. I know it's something I respond to when I read. That's the gratifying view. The other is that various people not supported, as I've never been, by a gang seek out others who wander about alone. At all events, there you are—by my own admission I'm a poets' poet. I've still not found the way out.

PR: With a few notable exceptions, these days the poets who are not poets' poets, or poets' poets' poets, as James Merrill called Elizabeth Bishop, are barely poets at all—and as the example of Bishop shows, going the distance as a writer admired by other writers is not an impossible route to sustained interest in the work. Helen Vendler herself led me to understand once that she thinks it is the poets who make traditions of attention by finding value in their seniors, although she doesn't of course always write as if powerful critics like herself had no say in the matter.

O'Brien seems to assume that the non-modern or non-post-modern types don't much understand what those experimental creatures are up to, which helps to simplify the picture by seeming to dole out the territory to two mutually uncomprehending tribes—with your work as a sort of Cresseid passed back and forth between the Greeks and the Trojans, or worse, suspended between them like M. Valdemar in Poe's story and *A Furnace*.

A problem with the gratifying view you give above might be that it suggests that the poets are all Rilke-like narcissists staring into the pool of your volumes and finding ripply reflections of their own faces there. I over-characterise, but not perhaps all that much. My question was more about the way the picture of poetic activities over the last three decades tends to get split up into exclusivities, as on the back of your Bloodaxe *New and Selected*: 'The reputation he gained in the 60s and 70s as a difficult poet is wrong: this book shows that he is one of the funniest etc'. Leaving out 'Matrix' and 'The Cut Pages' helps with what 'this book shows', though *The Ship's Orchestra*, the *Interiors with Various Figures* and *A Furnace* are hardly even superficially a bundle of laughs. 'Let the Blurb be strong, / modest and true'—the copywriters in Newcastle upon Tyne seem to have only taken note of your poem's first line.

Whether intentionally or not, your strategies have resisted pigeon-holing, as is clear enough to anyone comparing the blurb with the contents, and I'm struck by the example this offers, not as a set of options which individuals have colonised, digging in to exploit their chosen bit, but as an openness to deploying a repertoire of strategies for the different creative occasions that occur. Looking back, were there moments when you consciously resisted setting yourself up with a highly-defined signature style, and the baggage of exclusions and inclusions that might have gone with it?

RF: Somewhere in there you've located, very well, what I do. I might even suspect you of a little pond-gazing in pursuit of interests of your own, since I take you to be expert in ridding your poems of superfluous style-marks in order to keep the channel clear.

The idiot bipartite map isn't merely a British phenomenon. I just had a letter from August Kleinzahler complaining that he's going through a patch of being blamed by both sides for selling out to the other. Which shows what sort of game—a sideshow, an energy-drain—it all is. If you're positioned as I am between what I've described as those two turgid and uninviting whirlpools you go through periods of being unremarked by either (safe but potentially mortal) blamed by both (tedious) or accepted by both (embarrassing). The perpetual recurrence of the binary split gives the game away: the scene's not reducible in that way. A head-count would probably show that the majority of us live in the middle, outnumbering the ends.

PR: I'm trying to catch a difference in the experience of reading, say, Stevens or Yeats, or Larkin from about 1950 to 1977, where if you take against the manner you've got a serious problem about continuing at all, or reading a swathe of Fisher, where I suspect that someone who didn't find it easy to go on would not be in trouble with the manner—I'm not sure there is just one—but something more elusive, or dispersed, a whole set of inclinations and reluctances that have not solidified into one decided way of proceeding. If there are changes, as with, say, Yeats, your average important poet tends to have two or three 'periods' at most, with huge crises (like Auden 1938-42) and heaves from one style to another in between them.

RF: I see what you mean about phases of development, and very interesting that is. It seems to go with the early establishment of a 'successful' or recognisable manner which, having set, has to be cast periodically in favour of something that will fit a different size or shape of the writer. My first manner was neither early nor successful, so the question never arose. I've simply been continuously occupied with trying to get the same self down accurately. I'm not interested in development. The self-portrait I played with over 30 years ago in 'The Memorial Fountain' would, along with the writing exercises in which it's set in the poem, serve just as well today.

PR: Your apparent lack of these markers does seem quite unusual in a poet, where market forces too, or illusions about them, influence poetic styles through the expectation of a single 'voice' or a 'USP'—as Malcolm Bradbury is said to have encouraged his fiction students to develop—a 'unique selling point'! How did this kind of strait-jacketing fail to happen with you?

RF: As for the suppression of signature-marks, I've not done that in order to be anonymous, or a master of disguise, but merely to clean out features I consider to be toxins. Decoration—barring the occasional canter—elaboration, arguing the toss, questions, Personal Predicaments, loquacity, solemn or smart-ass closures of the 'I won the poem!' variety, and so on. One reason for my sometimes being occasionally to the taste of the modernist end may be that while I often start methodically and patiently I very rarely end in any such fashion: that would be real poison.

I suspect it's partly the biographers, veins full of chronology, who get us thinking in terms of development and periods. I'm not denying the presence of that element in artists' work; merely saying that it's too easily foregrounded. I'll have developed in the course of forty years—a cook goes in and out of focus many times as he learns—but not, I think, in periods, one supplanting another. For one thing, my work has been very intermittent, partly through occasional strong inbuilt inhibitory processes as in the late 1960s, partly through my perverse and persistent failure to set up a style of life that would look after it. And I realise I've a habit of regarding whatever work I happen to be engaged on as atypical, perpetually shelving the question of what something typical of me might be.

PR: You say you're not interested in development. But I imagine you'd admit to not being quite who you were when *City* was being written in the late fifties? I recall vividly as a culture-vulture teenager (the adjective is my father's) seeing Henry Moore on TV talking about how he never paid any attention to beauty. Beauty is a by-product, he said, of attending to something else. Is development another of those areas where you only really get it if you don't try for it, or pay any attention to it, I wonder?

Similarly, in 'Last Poems', you seem to touch on another instance of useful creative non-attending: 'But in all those years before / what *was* his subject?' I'm reminded of Vittorio Sereni describing his embarrassment if someone should unwittingly ask him what his thematics or themes were. He wasn't aware of having any, or could only talk about them as in specific instances of works already written. Is the uncertainty of the poet, to borrow a title of de Chirico's, something hapless or quietly cultivated? Is it even exactly 'uncertainty'?

RF: 'Last Poems'—I'm not sure what that little sketch of people looking at something they can't ask questions about has said, for it's a moment's intuition which I caught as best I could. But there's certainly a period in there, and an elusiveness. Your remarks about Moore and Sereni match my own experience completely; and if we want a more systematised Zen archery view of it we can go again to Cage. It seems to me the purest sense (and certainly something to be quietly cultivated) if you want to add something new to the world, not to go looking for it straight ahead, among the languages of identification. It's more likely to be walking with you, slightly behind and to one side, having been occupied in making itself out of what you know, but without your knowledge. Hawkeye tricks, like halting without warning on the off-chance it may lurch past you and into view, are customary. I've told how rare it has been for me to address already-known material directly. 'I saw what there was to say and I said it' &c ('Diversions'). In *A Furnace* I shied off making a structure of my own that might have turned out symmetrical, bottom-heavy and lethal, using instead the oblique strategy of seeding each section with something from Powys, a quotation, an impression, a theme, and letting each of them attract whichever of my materials seemed to go with them best.

PR: In an autobiographical essay, you mention writing your first poem in 1949, 'a pledge of allegiance to early Dylan Thomas, and every word of it was false'. Was his the first contemporary poetry you encountered?

RF: Oh, Edith Sitwell. Emphatically not anybody's Ph.D. topic, this; but ranging back and forth over time as we've been doing has suddenly brought up a remote memory. At school—I'll have been fifteen—I was confronted on a test paper with an unseen poem for comment: the usual formula of no identifying marks and the assumption that the piece is so out of the way that candidates won't have seen it (I've lived to see my own work turned to this use). It was the first modernist poem I'd ever seen. It was 'Jane, Jane, tall as a crane' from *Façade*. I can't say I took to it, and my comments were doubtless stuffy, even allowing for my natural Brummagem assumption that the crane was an item of heavy lifting gear. But I can remember the shock of recognising that I was seeing language used, not in pursuit of the seamless lucidity I was being trained to use, but as a device (with its stun-dart lexis and Steinian hammerings) for alternately concealing and revealing meaning. I read the rest of her earlier things with some interest. About the same time I caught sight in a corner of the Art room, of a small print: *Arlequin au Violon* by one Picasso. Never heard of him either. Same insight though.

PR: My Sitwell-type experience is a bit more shaming; at S-level the wise old examiners set 'Dry Loaf' without attribution, and I don't suppose that at 18 I had even heard the name Wallace Stevens so much as mentioned. I gave the poem a right dressing down, only to discover a few years later who I had been slagging off (with my handful of homemade, inappropriate aesthetic criteria). But since we've been talking about the uneasily humorous aspects to how poems can be used by the institutions of education, tell me, in 'The Making of the Book', were you consciously echoing Auden's 'For poetry makes nothing happen' with 'For poetry, we have to take it, is essential, / though menial'?

RF: No, Auden didn't speak into my ear, though Chaucer did in the closing lines, for some reason. Earlier in the poem I was fully absorbed in the persona I'd adopted and was possessed by his world view as revealed to me. Not in a holy trance, but in most review columns of the mid-sixties.

The immediate occasion was a sneering review in one of the Sundays of Christopher Middleton's *Nonsequences*. It was bad to see work that embodied knowledge, curiosity, invention and obvious talent—and for which there might at that time have been a public—having to submit itself to an ambush-gorge where the critical language didn't rise above terms like 'tiresome', 'irritating', 'predictable', 'pretentious'. The sixth-formers in charge seemed to think it was all good fun; but as I understand it it was things of that sort which had helped Middleton on his way to Texas.

PR: Well, then, let me ask you something about some of the poet figures who appear in *A Furnace*. There's the passage in which you refer to 'teachers / with passed-on clothes and a little Homer, / a little Wordsworth, two or three / generations of Symbolist poets'. I'm interested in the last of this list: would three generations of Symbolist poets reach to someone born in, say, 1930? Is the section a sort of self-portrait? Or a sardonic portrait of others? Then there are the lines I picked out for an epigraph over a decade ago: 'between / province and metropolis, / art and art, fantasy / and amenity' which come at the end of a section that begins 'There can be quaint cultures / where a poet who incurs exile / will taste it first'. Is this another self-portrait: the figure spending half a life puzzling 'at the statues in the town park...afterwards, fame and disgrace'?

RF: *A Furnace* III returns to the period of *City* and characterises the way the business of being called to pay attention, to learn, to find orientation, had seemed to me to be operating at that time. So there are quick sketches—I didn't want to conjure more than the shadowiest of presences, and certainly didn't want to be analytical—of myself and others like me, and also a wider range of types, sensed, observed, or found in the past. The category 'parsons' sons with dishevelled wits' could certainly include the Powys brothers—I didn't have any others in mind. The portraits aren't intended as sardonic.

   You've nailed me with the Symbolist poets. My quick sketch was too hasty to be arithmetically tidy, not quick enough to get away unexamined. Characterising the rough and ready un-smart learning of me and my sort, I chose to set down an impression of what it was like to start with Baudelaire and read on about as far as Valéry. Rather short generations.

   The class of poets who spend half a lifetime in hometown puzzlement—never mind what happens afterwards—isn't designed for my use alone. I'd put William Carlos Williams in it, and Larry Eigner, and quite a few Americans, by general artistic disposition. I'm at home in it, obviously. But the passage isn't meant to draw formal attention to me as an individual, inside or outside the poem, or both.

   As for 'fame and disgrace', I was turning over in my mind what seems to me a two-sided coin—quite speculatively, for I've never experienced fame. There are some tight paradoxes thereabouts, such as the way in which an aversion to a writer who becomes popular outside the circles of discrimination gets deepened by a sense of distaste for the public's acts of acceptance: a product of the beleaguered condition of the art.

PR: You occasionally deploy an 'I' in *A Furnace*, a fairly sustained one in the 'Introit' and then intermittently elsewhere. Was that a strategic decision or the result of local tactics? Does the fact that it only makes rare appearances in the poem suggest that for you it is not a necessity?

RF: The use of 'I' in *A Furnace* II is essential, but not systematic. In the 'Introit', where its first occurrence is designed to be emphatic, it was important for me to appear in the classical role of witness—Lucius Apuleius, say—somebody who recounts things which may well be his own inventions or metaphors, but who nevertheless is to be taken as stable and reliable. Much of the poem is concerned with summary and generalisation and I, as a character, progressively withdraw. Or so I notice. The strategy wasn't a conscious one. My character is present a good deal in Part I, necessarily, since it has to experience certain disturbances. Later, it's no more than an occasional pronoun among the traffic of the poem. Infinitive or participial constructions get used to signal the occasional surfacing or close proximity of the character. In III, for instance, he's constantly around, but in retrospect and without stability, and isn't accorded a pronoun. You may have spotted a few first-person plurals, in I and markedly in VI. Again, not by design. I think they're wish-signals, floated in the hope that if I pretend I'm not completely alone in my solipsism I may turn out not to be.

On reflection I can't see that I have a general policy about I, we and you in the poems, except, for instance, in 'Of the Empirical...' and 'The Poet's Message', where the thing is just being hauled up and kicked around to squash a few of the sleeping assumptions out. I do, I know, have a teeth-gritted, non-juror's, antinomian disinclination to speak in a poem (except for the wistful instance above) for the other member or members of a we/us or for a you. I don't like having anybody else doing my thinking for me or telling me what I may be presumed to think, feel, need or fear, so I've come, in writing, to bite back anything that might bring me into that sin. Maybe I overdo it. It's a personal thing, not an artistic principle—except insofar as I believe those pronouns, while looking innocuous, have a great potential for soaking energy from the surrounding language-field, much in the way Bunting had it in for adjectives: 'adjectives drain nouns'.

Risking self-contradiction, though, I have to come at it from another direction as well, and say that the foregoing describes a disinclination only. I'd never—and this is a principle—demand the exclusion or anathematisation of any feature of natural language, particularly conversation. Plenty of formally interesting poetry shunts itself by design into the presentation of sheets of individual but grammatically depersonalised sensibility in one mandarin idiolect or another. Identities and reputations have been built in this way. One should be aware of that paradox.

PR: You articulate a Scylla and Charybdis of pronouns pretty sharply here: if you leave them all out, or use them as strictly dramatic projections, the result is frequently a high-mandarin egomania in which everything refers back to the one subject whose verbal traces have apparently been expunged; if you put them in so as to parcel out the language and conceptual space to a series of characters (I, you, he, she, we, you, they) including the authorial 'personaggio', as the Dante in the poem is called by the Italians, then you may well get a dilution of verbal intensity, and, a thing that bothers some self-important readers, the sense that such readers are more than half-excluded from the

126

overheard verbal exchanges that are making up the poem. Do you think that the present states of the art have intensified these sorts of dilemma?

RF: Most of the present states of the art, insofar as I know them, seem under strain from the etiquettes of explicit and implicit authorship. I take it to be a persisting product of the grisly tango in which the pioneers of Modernism and their rich and discriminating patrons inevitably danced each other away from the sodden state consensus-readership had—again inevitably—got itself into. Which leaves us all out here where we find ourselves, like it or not. Some of us try to tunnel a way 'back' to some guessed-at location; some hang in and refine.

I'd always assumed that the post-medieval/pre-modern argument about authorial identity had been rapidly worked through to a usable conclusion about eighty years ago when Duchamp picked it up and ran with it. After which all artists needed at least to take stock of where on the scale from Promethean heroics to ostensibly anonymous presentations of chance findings they intended to work.

I was surprised when I realised around 1960 that the whole show was being run again for the benefit of everybody who missed it the first time, couldn't profit from the original documents or still couldn't believe it all. The re-run, of course, has been partly for the benefit of the Academy, which has turned a mostly honest penny reprocessing ideas for its extensive prepared public. I've been known, of course, for getting some of my techniques from old-time Modernism—montage, collage, basic cinematics and so forth. I've known that all along. Pragmatically, those things have suited me, and I've certainly felt no pull towards the mystiques of early Modernism; nor have I hankered after the ambience—not that it would ever have taken me to itself. The thought of the patrons makes my flesh creep.

PR: In a recent *Poetry Review* article you were quoted as suggesting that young poets should study Blake's 'If the fool would persist in his folly he would become wise'. That 'Proverb of Hell' is also alluded to in *A Furnace*. Could you elaborate on what it's doing in the poem? Are you just telling the young poets to write and write, even if it looks like disaster?

RF: Blake's proverbs are at least ambiguous, but in the context of a question about the sort of preparation young writers should give themselves the strand I stressed was the idea that singularity was something to protect, even if it showed itself as gauche, self-strangling or embarrassing. These days, once you've chosen your idiom, there are paths to conformity waiting. If you want to inhabit the poetry competition world you can find somebody who'll teach you to maximise your poem, turn it into a gunboat bristling with closures or an arrangement of managed tones; if you stand aloof from that sort of thing you can get guidance on how to write smooth copy with no protuberances that could trigger the booby-traps that would label you unregenerate.

PR: In the first of 'Four Songs from the Camel's Coffin', you write of how 'Lost / lives, lost voices, blanked-out / patches of myself now all / of a kind together have all gone into the world'. That seems not to be the 'world of light' in the Henry Vaughan poem your phrase recalls. I'm struck by the idea of them as having become part of the world, like those additions to the stock of available reality that R. P. Blackmur, was it?, called poems. Have you found that persisting with poetry has seemed like painting yourself into a corner surrounded by your cemetery of performance, statues of it built everywhere?

RF: That cemetery of performance was less of a settled vision than a passing thought I had forty-odd years ago, when I hadn't actually done anything much at all. Maybe I was giving myself a safety-net. I don't look at my own writings, additions to the world, if you like, or hear them in my head, enough to feel crowded by them.

I can't begin to paraphrase my truncated quotation from Vaughan, though my 'world' is obviously not his world of light. It was lying there waiting to be picked up when I reached that point in the poem, which was already behaving like a Möbius strip. So in Vaughan's beginning was my end.

This edited conversation was conducted via e-mail between Earl Sterndale, England, and Sendai, Japan, from April to June 1998.

Roy Fisher

on

Roy Fisher

When Roy Fisher was lying paralysed in hospital for much of last year, unable to do more than collaborate distantly with Andrew McAllister of Bloodaxe on the preparation of *The Dow Low Drop*, he bound himself, so it's said, by a great oath: to refrain from writing any book of poems about lying paralysed in hospital. 'Why should I become rich and famous?' he'd say. If this story is true, it illustrates and exposes the sustained diffidence of the man once referred to by Peter Porter as 'the excellent Roy Fisher, whom no one suggested should be made Poet Laureate'. Given profitable copy by a malign fate, it was quite in character for Fisher, selflessly or through arrogance, to leave the field clear for similarly afflicted people of the sort who write in the broadsheets. As for the Laureateship, he was among those who—at its change of tenant in 1984— were recommending its abolition on the grounds that it brought the art into disrepute and ridicule.

An approving review of one of Fisher's early books. wrote: 'Insofar as Fisher can be said to have a subject .... it has to be the Provinces'. In the face of a welcome like that, Fisher can probably be forgiven for going instantly to ground and conducting the remainder of his public career from various positions of concealment, his manoeuvrings occasionally revealed as he moves from one patch of cover to another. The elusiveness probably had a much longer history. In his essay in the *Contemporary Authors Autobiography Series* (reprinted in this volume as 'Antebiography') he tells how for years in his tough Birmingham primary school he kept himself in one piece only by being 'The Daft Kid', too much of an idiot to be fun to beat up, though all the while surreptitiously coming top in schoolwork. Open self-assertion and proselytising conviction seem to be faculties he was born without, and his merits as a writer come by a different route: although he's not personally reclusive it's impossible to imagine Fisher ever burning to set up a reading-series, issue a manifesto, edit a magazine or a didactic anthology, or solicit an opportunity to barnstorm schoolchildren into admiring his meticulous, low-key accounts of Breton ossuaries. His work appears to have come about almost entirely in response to outside initiatives. He habitually publishes, and, one suspects, even writes, only when pressed, as if feeling a need to keep his flying hours up and his accreditation open.

Late starter

He was a late starter in any case He was over thirty before his first pamphlet, *City*, appeared and a further six years passed before there was a book, *The Ship's Orchestra*, by which time he was well into a writer's block, which was to last him until 1970, its end coinciding with his emergence from an intermittently haunted and phobic period of his life. All the same, Fisher has now been on the scene for a long while. By various shifts and dedicated efforts his writings have been progressively collected and kept in print almost without lapse for thirty-five years. Even so, it apparently hasn't always been easy for people to get a clear view of what he's been up to. From the first there's been a tendency to sideline him as being probably somebody else's baby. For years he was described as having his reputation-needs taken care of by Americans; or he was a painter masquerading as a writer; or a jazz musician straying into words and out again. The *TLS* review of his 1980 interim *Collected* appeared in print shorn by editorial cartography of the reviewer's original assumption that the work existed in the same world—heterodox enough, you might think—as that of the Faber Four of the time, Larkin, Gunn, Hughes, Heaney (none of them, incidentally, appreciably greedier for celebrity than Fisher). The map left him, as before, in charge of his own off-shore island in the middle of England, hung in deep international space somewhere off Spaghetti Junction. In recent years the style has been to commend him warmly and for the right reasons, while remarking on his inexplicable neglect—'an offence against public decency' as *Bête Noire* grandly called it.

The Dow Low Drop—the title's taken from a still-fragmentary long sequence based on a monstrous quarry-scar near his home—is in the main a very substantial *Selected* which makes the greater part of his work available again, more clearly and approachably arranged than previously. The selection includes, uncut, the sequences 'City', 'Wonders of Obligation', 'It Follows That', 'Metamorphoses', and the fictional (one hopes) 'Interiors With Various Figures' and also two complete books: *The Ship's Orchestra* and *A Furnace;* the latter, for all its unconscious or unashamed solipsism, one of the most ambitious recent English poems I've read. These works take up, as they should, almost two thirds of the book, and the fact illustrates something consistent in Fisher's approach. With no gift for the anecdotal-discursive, self-contained, teachable A4 poem, he's happiest at the extremes of duration: the three-or-four-line fragment or the forty-page long haul, And this takes us to the heart of what he's about. I think he's a Romantic, gutted and kippered by two centuries' hard knocks. The willingness to regard his sketch-books as exhibitable ('Diversions', 'It Follows That') and to go on shamanic mental trips though humdrum-looking material are the indicators. Either way, the technique is one of epiphanic revelation. He doesn't judge his material; he lets it judge him, in the form of his ability to perceive and render it. If he can't see anything he can't say anything. There's a considerable and, I should guess, carefully-preserved naïveté at work here.

Laconic endings

This watch-and-wait approach probably gives a better explanation of his disinclination to predict the course of a poem or to structure perorations than does the usual one that it's something brought across from his work as a jazz musician. The jazz link is most likely a matter of style and tone, in that he's a poet of insidious openings, occasional sustained flights and laconic endings, signs which mark a few genres of jazz music rather than the radical theory of instant improvisation, which isn't, of course, peculiar to jazz. And other forms of music have their place in the poetry: in a radio interview, for instance, Fisher once described the contribution Shostakovich's flayed clarity had made to his treatment of the dead in *A Furnace*.

Fisher's an effective phrase-maker, and he'd be eminently quotable, if only anybody could find a reason to quote him. The tone is habitually exact and unexcited, and he's obviously a writer who tugs the seams of his syntax to see if they hold. (The satires are exceptions: there the material's slung down happily just as it comes, and is the better for it.) Mostly he makes little distinction between verse and prose—one of his favourite line-forms is in fact a series of very short prose paragraphs—and he moves with equal ease in both. By contrast, the very few examples of his critical prose and reviewing to reach print show signs of struggle. Given a subject to address, he grows adjectival and simile-ridden, with dependent clauses cramming themselves into the sentences wherever they can, like piglet runts scrambling to find an unsucked dug. He clearly prefers freedom.

Abstemious

Occasionally in the poems, though, he'll let himself get trapped, almost as if on purpose, into a corner where the only way out is by using one of the grand abstractions. At such points he's capable of turning on the poor word as if resentfully, treating it as opaque, a stray item from other people's language. There's a curious parallel here with the jazz pianist Joe Sullivan, with whose intensely emotional and declamatory playing Fisher admits to having been obsessed since boyhood. Sullivan, alcoholic and of uncertain temper, would sometimes impatiently belabour his own music, often by spastic repetitions, as if frustrated by the limitations of his medium. He's an interesting allegiance in any case for the notoriously emollient and abstemious Fisher, on whom the considered verdict of the Contained Cambridge School, sent across country by messenger some days after he'd first read there, ran: 'He only drank a pint and a half all night'. The same town brought out the emollience, too: it's recorded that when the organisers of the Cambridge Poetry Festival invited participants to list others with whom they wouldn't appear, Fisher was the only one to send in a nil return. There are, indeed, grounds for suspecting that Fisher has never learned enough about his fellow poets to understand why he should dislike them. (Certainly he's always been happier to be out fighting the jazz-club pianos of his beloved Provinces.)

Several commentators have noted uneasily that the list of things Fisher's poetry omits to mention has to include social optimism; and that omission, combined with his willingness to invoke and inspect images of awe, pomp and intimidation, leads them into wondering whether there isn't maybe a covert political nostalgia for that sort of thing. The evidence all points the other way. Fisher's political disposition is plain enough to see: it constantly breaks the surface of *A Furnace*, though never programmatically and is generally apparent once recognised. Nostalgia has no part in it. I take him to be an anarchist who simply has no time whatever for hierarchical systems, monotheisms or state authority; or for capitalism, along with the absorbent, malleable selves it breeds and with which it populates its democracies and its literatures. For Fisher the world ruled by such rackets is nevertheless the only world, into which everybody's born already swimming or going under. He's about as right-wing as Luis Buñuel.

From Fisher's previously collected work this *New and Selected* omits half a dozen sizeable sequences, some lesser ones and sixty or seventy single poems, as well as the extended prose work *The Cut Pages* from 1971 (republished jointly in 1985 by Oasis and Shearsman) and the 1994 collection *Birmingham River*. So there's a volume of some weight in prospect when all these texts are gathered together. Your reviewer, for one, hopes that book won't be so long delayed as to be a Posthumous Collected.

Talks for Words

Roy Fisher

ONE

I'm improvising this talk into a cheap cassette recorder. Or rather, I was. By the time you hear it I shall have transcribed and typed it: the typescript will have been retyped by the BBC and I shall have read it back into a more sophisticated recording machine. Indeed, that's what I'm doing now. But also what I'm doing now is possibly something which won't be caught on the tape at all: I may be switching on my car radio to hear my own voice coming up past my knees, and talking about doing so as it does so.

But now I'm sitting at home a couple of weeks ago, talking into my cassette recorder, and thinking of this moment, a week or so ahead, when I'm reading what I'm saying into another recorder; and this moment a week or so more ahead, when you're listening—and maybe I am too.

There's a certain sacrilege in talking like this. It's not so long since a recorded programme was thought of as somehow *ersatz*, and I'm certainly not asking you to consider the complex business of reproducing sounds in any technical sense. But I do find it remarkable that to store and transmit words as trivial as these with even so mall a degree of sophistication sets the little bits of material I'm using into a variety of different time scales, like dropping corks into a river with varying currents, so that the nows that I'm talking about—and of course as I talk at this minute there are three or four of them present, in my mind—are moving through my ordinary empirical sense of time at different rates, and with different physical surroundings; and yet the ostensible text is one and the same.

To have these not very important bits of material floating through your life over a period of two or three weeks on these different time scales, going into and coming out of these different boxes, is rather strange, and it reminds me of a day years ago when the looseness of the fit between ideas and texts was brought home to me strongly. I'd just been put in charge of a large class of not very able ten-and-eleven-year-olds, and one of the first things I asked them to do was write a story. At the end we had a session in which some of them read their work out. One boy at the back was frantic to let us hear what held done. He jumped up and read, running his forefinger along the lines, something that went like this: "It was totally dark in the cave as we entered. Bradly paid out the rope, taking care not to snag it on the projecting spurs of rock; and as we took our last look at the daylight we all wondered how long it would be before any of us saw it again. We advanced down the damp glistening floor of the tunnel. I could see our leader's light bobbing ahead in the gloom, and so on. This was a good deal better than I'd been led to expect, and I went over to look at his book. As I approached him he went rather pink, and made a lot of busy movements. The page had nothing but a brief jumble of incoherent marks—and, indeed, he was virtually illiterate. But the limitations of script weren't getting between him and his concentration on his brilliant piece of bluff.

There was another boy, rather slower, less ingenious who was also illiterate; but in his case it was preposterous to use that word, because the one thing he could do was form letters beautifully, but without knowing what they meant. He'd learned a very careful and elegant italic hand, in which he could write his own name, and any combination of letters that gave him manual and visual pleasure in writing.

He was less eager to read, because he knew that what his hand bad written wasn't a guide to the words he'd thought, and he had less gift for extemporising. But when I looked at his page, it was a beautiful piece of lettering, clean and even. His favourite letter combinations were those containing a gh; and if you read his piece aloud it would go: 'EGHECHI - EGHEGH - ECEOGHI - EGHIGIII - ONCEGH'. He couldn't. of course, read back the sounds I've just made; but being literate, I can. Indeed, I've no alternative.

Now, as I said when I started, at some stage in the transmission of these ideas to you from my original tape, I shall have transcribed them, and the typist will have retyped then very clearly for me to read. But at this moment there's something only the producer, the typist and I know. And that's whether the script I'm reading from is one in which I let the typist do the whole script using only her own favourite five letters on the keyboard; or whether it's one in which I insisted she confine herself to my favourite three.

TWO

Alex Comfort, in *Sex and Society*, coined the intriguing phrase 'adulterous prop'. This simply describes the function of those long-suffering, or short-suffering, individuals who help to keep somebody else's marriage going by diverting one of the partners from his or her boredom or misery. Years ago I watched a *Man Alive* feature about a brisk and jolly lady whose chosen role was to be, over and over again, just such a prop—the perpetual Other Woman. She obviously plied her hobby with deftness and style, but one thing she said was chilling. It went something like this. 'And just when they're feeling satisfied and mumbling nice things with their eyes shut, I lean over them on the pillow, and make them look at me. What is my name? I say, What's my name?', She particularly enjoyed it when they got it wrong. This was shown at the time when you couldn't help being reminded of the voice of Muhammad Ali, slamming Ernie Terrell round the ring to the sound of those same words, when Terrell had taunted him under his discarded name of Cassius Clay.

It must be a fine thing to have some stability in your name, some sense that it identifies you, even if you've had to alter it to reach a satisfying effect. When I was a boy I was relieved for a time to have escaped being called Walter, after my father, or Barnabas, after the saint whose day I was born on; but later I might have been glad to have had either in place of the weak flavourless monosyllable I was given. In the accents of my native town it had a little character, in that it came out as Rye; but when people started getting it right it seemed a complete cipher, hard to live down to.

In fact, it was many years before I really had to accept it. I lived first through a series of applied names, all of which seemed appropriate at the time: The Bab; Fatty; Podgy; Fish. When I was quite small strangers would look at me and say 'Howdo, George!' and I thought there must be some truth in that, if I looked like a George even at first sight. And most people who knew perfectly well who I was would call me by the name of my quite different older brother. I suppose that while I was making instantaneous translations of what made sense to them into what made sense to me I was learning to expect a profound discontinuity between names and things.

Later, when I was a schoolmaster I once had an experience which made me feel I was hearing my most real name. I was approaching a rowdy classroom. The lookout boy saw me coming, rushed into the room, and I heard him cry 'Ssh! Here comes—' and he said a name. I didn't hear it perfectly; it sounded like Snafty or Slafty. I'd never heard it before, and I didn't bother to ask what it had been, because I knew I wouldn't get a true reply, but I felt I'd heard the name I was really known by—and there's no name more binding than a teacher's nickname. I did, however, as a teacher, have a name I was happier with than with most of my names. I was Sir, just used as a proper noun, not as a title. 'I'll tell Sir!' In my mind I spelled it like a French reflexive, se—s.e. It seemed the proudest, freest, most self-regarding name you could have.

After the ontological insecurity brought on by my own unstable naming, the naming of both my sons was carried out on the principle of combining certitude with flexibility. Each was given a first name suitable for a life of rough and ready likeability; a second name suited to a career of relentless social climbing; and a third to be used in the event of advanced narcissistic decadence. Both boys took immediately to their first names and stuck to them, and probably will do so even if their lives came to belie the labels.

For my part, I live now openly under my given names, but in a place called Larchwood, which is not a larch wood, but a large grassy square with a few deodars at one end, to lend conviction.

THREE

Saul Steinberg once made a famous series of drawings of people's speech, in which a succession of talking heads emitted visual equivalents of their speech characteristics—from one, a cloud of birds; from another, a bouquet of flowers, from another, an ornate building; from another, tangles of what looked like horsehair—and you knew, without a single word being referred to, just what language personality each of these people had. The heads were characterised so that you could see how appropriate what came out of each mouth was; and indeed the patterns were expressions of personality—personal offerings. They needn't have been anything to do with speech at all; they could have been designs for personalised wallpaper or dress fabrics. But the fact that Steinberg chose to link then to the act of speaking brings out two points that are interesting. One is that by making a graphic description of language he's by-passing the almost inevitable air of pedantry which comes over anybody who sits down to talk solemnly about anything so mercurial as language; and the other is that his firm linking of language to individuality seems to assume that some of us at least live in quite personal worlds of language. It's as if the people in the drawings had borrowed, or leased, the makings of their language from a common stock, but had used that stock—what we usually call 'the language'—merely as a basis for rich personal variations, much as people buy mass-produced cars and immediately set to to redesign them out of all recognition.

Steinberg's being a caricaturist and not a linguist; and he's not propounding a general rule. The drawings I've mentioned do put an exaggerated stress on idiosyncrasy. If you put the horsehair, the birds, the blossoms, the buildings together and didn't say what they represented, they wouldn't have much in common.

In reality, of course, the idiosyncratic elements in anybody's speech or writing constitute only a minute proportion of it, but it acts like a drop of concentrated flavouring, dispersing itself through the whole. And we're able to respond to it very sensitively, just as we respond to the extremely complex information-sorting which we do when we recognise somebody's face, and know it from all other faces. I can think now of the talk of people I've not heard for many years, some of them long since dead, and with their voices unrecorded. But to say what I think, how I'm able to remember them, is very difficult. I can only put it in some such way as this—I can say, for example, 'I can imagine my grandfather talking.' I certainly don't get an auditory hallucination, that is, I don't hear a voice; I don't even get a sense that distinguishable words or messages are being uttered. But I do have, still ready for use, though it's been in storage since his death more than thirty years ago, a configuration of disembodied tones, inflections, turns of phrase—the recognition-kit for that individual language that was my grandfather's. And I suppose that although I shall never need to use it again in its own right, since I shall never hear its owner again, I'm still referring to it from time to time as part of my general orientation towards new voices I'm learning.

A biologist would make his own sort of comment on this hypertrophy of our ability to distinguish among other individuals of our own species on a minutely detailed level; what interests me is how we use it socially. We're all familiar with self-appointed word-watchers who position themselves along the sea wall ready to raise the flood alarm if they hear a single syllable slip; and many of us have had the uncomfortable experience of finding we think less well of a friend who makes a spelling mistake, even though we know the spelling rule's both illogical and ridiculously demanding. It's easy to be over-sensitised to the signals.

I can say this even though I come from Birmingham, a place which is popularly supposed to be the home of the utmost linguistic crudity; a place whose inhabitants are believed to have brass throats, gaping mouths full of grit, and cloth ears since if they could hear themselves they wouldn't speak the way they do. The local accent's one nobody ever wants to acquire; even actors and comedians hardly ever listen to it for long enough to learn more than its simplest features. In fact, though, in terms of the subtleties of English pronunciation and usage, it's a region of perpetual muffled fighting, a borderland between the embattled North and the complacent South. Or rather, since the military metaphor has too much of commitment about it, it's a human market place where market forces rule; where successive generations of the same family will have different accents; where members of the same household will choose their accents and maintain them or modify then without attracting any great attention to themselves thereby; where individuals will go beyond the ordinary bilingualism of work-speech and home-speech and take their language up-market and down-market again over different periods of their lives. The local language is fluid: its variations reflect personal status, aspiration or resignation more than any minor regional origins. I think it's more rarely than in other industrial cities that you'll find examples of the old language still showing through, archaic, against the tide: the little boy, left on his own on a playing field, crying miserably: 'Ah wor puk!' That is to say, 'I wasn't picked!' Unless he learns the language of the main chance, he won't be.

FIVE

Anybody who's ever been tongue-tied will know the enormous force of one's own silence. I'm not talking about extreme cases, like drying up on stage, with everybody waiting to hear your next word, when you can't even remember what a word is: I'm talking about silences which can be quite prolonged without attracting much attention at all. I teach for a living, which means that for a large part of the time I talk too much, having learned some sort of fluency by necessity. And sometimes in a group discussion I have to check myself and reflect that somebody who has volunteered nothing, yet isn't obviously asleep or writing a letter, may well be undergoing an experience I've often had. This consists of following the conversation of several other people, quite actively, but at a slight remove in time, so that the conversation always slightly outpaces you, as if it were being relayed by satellite. You never lose touch with it, but the little time-lags you need for finding words are being withheld, or obstructed by somebody else who jumps in with something that takes the subject away from where you were. And unless you make an issue of wanting to speak, by calling a halt, or unless somebody does the same by calling directly on you to find your tongue, it's possible to spend an hour or two in company—some people obviously spend virtually their whole lives like this—with unspoken thoughts, half-verbalised; uncontributed contributions; and if they haven't spoken, then on a conversational scorecard they have scored zero, even though they have a considerable build-up of near-conversation. These words may be left swilling around in the head; and that brings with it very often the familiar sense of the language discharged later to oneself, the conversation—both sides of it—which never developed; the conversation there might have been.

This is a rebound-language which isn't being used, except for clarification, and these dead and frustrated bits of conversation are converted to one of the other uses of language, which is the language of introspection. I suppose anybody will use that language when devising something important; but of course some people must live very large parts of their mental lives, their linguistic lives, on this strange relayed level of crypto-conversation, I can remember times when language of that sort, rattling away in the head, jabbering away in my own ear, could blot out what I felt was the proper business of my mind. It would get between me and the world. The only virtue the experience had was to make me feel at least capable of sympathy for the plight of the policeman who comes to my door with a solemn, open, confidence-inspiring manner and maybe a serious message; but his message, to say nothing of his manner, always gets cut into by a strange strangulated parrot voice that suddenly comes squawking out of his chest from the radio-phone. He's learned to ignore it, but I can't.

There's one example of an interior, or internalised language which has always fascinated me, though I've never found it attractive. George Orwell would, for practice, verbalise any experience he had time to verbalise; that is, he would write it in his head as it was happening, would convert it into a realistic narrative; so that on entering a room he would 'render' it, like an artist sketching; he would imagine how it would need to read. I've never really wanted to try this: the verbal rendering of a scene is bound to be affected by the characterisation of whoever's looking at it. Orwell's eye and language would be different from Alain Robbe-Grillet's. I'd be wary of inwardly talking myself into the character of a know-all reporter who can find words for just about anything.

I started by talking about silence, the social silence of failing to start talking. Possibly a great deal of that failure can be blamed on our excessive respect for the delicate conventions of entering conversations. Not everybody conforms. I'll give just two examples of originality. Once I travelled a long way on a rainy night to hear a reading by a visiting American poet for whose work I had, and have, a great respect. Ushered into a hall of complete strangers, he had the demeanour of a man who was ready to start by saying how glad he was to be there, and so forth. The chairman welcomed him and withdrew, leaving him to introduce his reading. So far as my recollection goes, his first words were: "Notwithstanding, at all events, the significance of the attention as placed, towards with quote regard unquote location . . . . We were soon off in pursuit, but some felt winded from the start. The other example comes from the early career of a young man I know. He first showed he wasn't like everybody else at the age of about three, when he walked into a room full of people, looked penetratingly at the company, said, very clearly, 'Besides which!' and left. Besides which—

Long ago I formed the idea of becoming a poet by writing poems. I'd tried painting, and I'd tried music, but had been oppressed by the difficulty of avoiding academic training in these arts—an avoidance which at the time seemed to me essential. But it was a time when nobody in this country would have suggested that it was possible or desirable to teach imaginative writing beyond the rudiments of school composition, so my way was clear. My readings about poetry threw up very few prescriptions, and I was sorry rather than glad to find even those. I can remember struggling, rather unwillingly, to take to heart the warnings Wystan Auden issued in the preface of his selection from Tennyson. He said that if a young man came to him full of important things he wanted to say, then that young man would never be a poet; if, on the other hand, he said 'I like hanging around words, listening to what they say,' then maybe one day he would be a poet. I thought this a piece of rather mystical pedantry, but I saw the force of it. And it was probably my first acquaintance with the anthropomorphic view of language, the suggestion that it has a will of its own. It's one of those jokes that feeds off a real unease.

At any rate, I set about writing my poems, and kept at it. It was probably my own fault that the first twenty years weren't much fun; at any rate there was a moment after the first ten when dissatisfaction got the better of me and I dashed off a piece of self-mocking doggerel, in which the art of poetry figured as an insatiable nuisance, a hole in the floorboards into which I stuffed anything I could find, worthless or valuable, in an effort to stop the draught and get some peace. It ended like this:

> I prodded lengths of string
> down with a long pin,
> I fetched water and milk,
> and let them trickle in;
> lead shot, nail-parings, currants,
> torn-up paper bags,
> splinters that once were furniture
> my clothes cut into rags;
> and so, morsel by morsel,
> till its last trick was sprung,
> I poked my life away into
> the bland English tongue.

The mood that produced that piece has long since left me; but I can recreate quite easily the particular pleasure it gave me in the final line to turn and bite my own language—the bland English tongue. And that was the real target for my recriminations—not poetry itself, which still seemed a world of fine possibilities, but the language I had to write in, which I thought pallid and limp in its sounds and its structures. I'd been caught, of course, in the trap Auden had described. I'd been trying to make poems out of huge, fateful ideas, and had been greedily huffing and puffing at the language to make things happen. I had I suppose done my share of hanging around words listening to what they said, in terms of Auden's preferred course of action; but having listened to what they'd said, I'd thought it effete.

I'd been brought up to appreciate the rich resources of English as an expressive language, particularly from Chaucer onwards; to understand the huge range of its metaphoric and rhythmic potential, and the sinuousness of its syntax. On the shadier side I was also intimately familiar with the fiendish intricacies of the nuances of servility and dominance which it contributes to its ignoble alliance with our class-ridden society system. But for me the strength was a sunset glow, and the flexibility was the flexibility of a watch by Salvador Dali—the sort that drips over the edge of a chest of drawers like a strip of liver.

At any rate, that's how it seemed. I had too little faith, I wasn't ready to listen; and I recant. But I can't help regretting our socially-generated prevalence of deferential or diffident turns of phrase and speech tunes, or the loss from Standard English of some of the strongly-formed consonants the Scots and Northumbrians still have.

You can't play Canute with language. It must change; and if the changes don't match your purpose, then your work is that much the harder. I tend to take plenty of holidays into festive sub-languages just outside the city limits of English. Foreign film subtitles, for instance, with their continual tiny cliff-hangers in mid-sentence. Or the pithy names of German-American jazz musicians—the trumpeter Lyman Vunk, the drummer Kurt Bong, of the Oskar Doldinger Trio; or the early existentialist tuba player who was a member of Owen Fallon's Californians in 1925—one Hartmann Angst.

In the end, language has to be accepted, if with resignation. If I had been without language until this moment, and were offered it, I think might react as Samuel Beckett is reported to have done when they told him he'd won the Nobel Prize. 'It is a disaster,' he said; and took the money.

A Checklist of Interviews with Roy Fisher
compiled by Derek Slade

Sad Traffic 5, Barnsley, 1971, pp. 31-4. 'A Tuning Phenomenon: An Interview with Roy Fisher'. Interviewer unidentified.

Nineteen Poems and an Interview, Grosseteste Press, Pensnett, Staffs., June 1975, pp. 12-38. 'An Interview with Roy Fisher'. The interviewers are Jed Rasula and Mike Erwin. The interview is dated 19 November 1973.

Saturday Morning 1, London, Spring 1976, unpaginated. 'Conversation with Roy Fisher'. Transcript of a conversation between RF and Eric Mottram, 22 January 1973.

Granta 76, Cambridge, June 1977, pp. 17-19. 'Roy Fisher talks to Peter Robinson'.

Hack 1, Madeley College of Education, Crewe, 1980, pp. 16-34. 'Interview with Roy Fisher'. The interviewer is John Gallas. The interview took place in November 1980.

Gargoyle 24, Washington, D.C., 1984, pp. 75-96. 'Turning the Prism: An Interview with Roy Fisher'. The interviewer is Robert Sheppard. The interview took place on 7 June 1982. This was republished in chapbook form in 1986 by Toads Damp Press, London under the same title.

Arts Report: The Arts Newspaper of the West Midlands 53, June 1986, p. 10. 'And then back to Sparkbrook'. The intervewer is David Hart.

'*Interview: Roy Fisher by Helen Dennis*'. University of Warwick, 1987. Transcript of a conversation that took place on 9 May 1984.

'*John Tranter Interviews Roy Fisher*'. Published in two parts on the Internet by Jacket magazine at http://www.jacket.zip.com.au/jacket01/fisheriv.html. The interview took place on 27 September 1989.

Staple 18, Mickleover, Derbyshire, Summer 1990, pp. 41-6. 'Talking to *Staple*: Roy Fisher'. The interviewers are Donald Measham and Bob Windsor. The interview took place on 5 April 1990.

Brodsky Through the Eyes of his Contemporaries Valentina Polukhina, St. Martin's Press, 1992, pp. 292-307. This contains 'A Noble Quixotic Sight', an interview with RF by Valentina Polukhina about Joseph Brodsky. The material was reprinted, translated into Russian, in *Zrezda* no. 1: St Petersburg, 1997.

Prop 2, Bolton, Lancs., 1997, pp. 28-30. 'People who can't float'. The interviewer is Ra Page.

Poetry News: the Newsletter of the Poetry Society London, Spring, 1998, pp. 8-9. 'The cost of letters'. The interviewer is Siân Hughes.

"They Are All Gone into the World": Roy Fisher in Conversation with Peter Robinson. The interview was conducted via e-mail from April to June 1998. Printed for the first time in *Interviews Through Time, and Selected Prose* ed. Tony Frazer, Shearsman Books, Kentisbeare, Devon, 1999.

New from Stride Publications:

News for the Ear

a homage to Roy Fisher

edited by Robert Sheppard & Peter Robinson

Roy Fisher's poetry has clearly meant quite different things to many different people. This celebration of the seventieth birthday of its author is a hetereogenous affair, with a range of responses. Poets, from the well known and influential, such as Thom Gunn, August Kleinzhaler, and Charles Tomlinson, rub shoulders with others to whom the poetry of Roy Fisher has spoken. Peers such as Gael Turnbull and Lee Harwood, the Irish poet Maurice Scully and the Australian poet John Tranter, and many others, testify to his appeal in both poetry and prose. The volume contains new poems by Fisher and unpublished prose: a detailed account of his life as a Birmingham jazz musician. The volume concludes with a long interview which offers new perspectives on the work of one of the most important poets writing today.

Available, post free, for £8.95 [or $15 *bills only*] from:
STRIDE, 11 SYLVAN ROAD, EXETER, DEVON EX4 6EW
(Cheques payable to 'Stride' please]